PLANTS FOR
SMALL GARDENS

FRANCES WELLAND

This is a Parragon Book
This edition published in 2003

Parragon
Queen Street House
4 Queen Street
Bath BA1 1HE, UK

Conceived, edited, illustrated
and produced by Ditchfield Publishers

Cover Design by Bridgewater Books

ISBN 1-40540-479-5

A copy of the British Library Cataloguing in Publication
Data is available from the Library.

Typeset by Action Publishing Technology Ltd, Gloucester
Colour origination by Colour Quest Graghic Services Ltd,
London E9

Printed in China

Half title page: *Camellia japonica 'Elsie Jury'*
Frontispiece: *Tulipa 'White Triumphator'*
Title page: *Hedychium gardnerianum*
Contents page: *Fuchsia 'Dusky Blue'*

CONTENTS

INTRODUCTION

NEARLY ALL of us have small gardens today. This is usually from necessity because we live in towns or suburbs where, at the most, our dwellings typically have a square at the front and at the back, sometimes elongated into a rectangle. We might of course have less space at our disposal: a roof garden perhaps or a tiny patio or terrace. But whatever the area, in all these circumstances the garden becomes in effect another room (or two) of the house. It is a small, orderly, self-contained space for private escape from the public world.

Increasingly often, however, we have small gardens from choice. This is the case where owners of much larger gardens decide to subdivide their space into several smaller gardens. The argument for this treatment is that it makes the whole garden so much more interesting. It is always boring for the eye to see everything at a single glance. How much more intriguing to wonder what is behind the hedge or wall that conceals an individual enclosure or another garden room. Not only this, but it gives the gardener the opportunity as well to create separate areas with different moods and features.

Small gardens are therefore desirable, though they are equally a challenge to create. The reason for this is that there isn't the same room here for mistakes as there is in

OPPOSITE: Pots enable you to move plants to the most effective positions.

Large plants in a small space have impact and surprise.

a larger garden. Every single plant in a small space has got to earn its place. It needs to work harder: flower longer perhaps, or have good foliage, or be evergreen to clothe the space in winter. Most important, it has to be the right plant in the right position. And when the small garden is going to be seen in its entirety from the house at all seasons – which is usually the case – it is even more of a challenge to create. You have to rely on the right choice of plants as well as the structure of the design to keep it in consistently good form; and the only way to choose plants is to study your garden first.

ASSESSING THE SITE

It is impossible to choose plants without assessing the area which will be their home. This means taking account of its aspect (whether it faces north or south, for example); the times when it receives sun and shade; its windiness or shelter; the nature and quality of the soil. These facts dictate whether your plants thrive or fail.

Some of these facts will take quite long to establish, because they will only become evident as the seasons pass. Some parts of your garden for example are likely to be in shade at one time of the year, and in sun at others. This matters, because the timing of sun and shade affects some plants. Morning sun, for instance is disadvantageous to camellia flowers because sun on frosted petals will spoil the blooms. Alternatively, mid-day sun, when it is at its hottest, may be too excessive for other plants. Only a year's observation of your garden will give you this kind of detail.

ASSESSING AND PREPARING SOIL

Soil is either acid, neutral or alkaline, expressed in what is called the pH scale. Its acidity or alkalinity matters because lime-intolerant plants (such as rhododendrons, some heaths, camellias, etc.) will not thrive in an alkaline soil. You can buy soil-testing kits which will assess your soil type.

In other respects, certain soil-types are recognizable by their textures and should be treated accordingly. 1) Sandy soil is light, gritty and dries out quickly. Add peat or compost to improve its ability to hold moisture. 2) Chalky soil is shallow and sometimes has lumps of chalk or limestone in its subsoil. Add compost or rotted manure and fertilizers. 3) Clay soil is heavy and sticky in winter like plasticine, yet dries out in summer to concrete. Dig it over roughly in the autumn to allow frosts to break it down and add strawy compost or organic matter. If the clay is very heavy, it is possible to add garden lime over dry soil. Don't add any fertilizers for at least one month before liming and for three months afterwards. Also, liming means you cannot grow lime-intolerant plants in the soil, nor even in those areas into which the soil or water might leach to any extent.

THE PLANTS IN THIS BOOK

The plants here have been selected for every purpose. Many can be grown in containers whether tubs, hanging baskets or pots of all kinds. Many of the plants are evergreen to keep the garden dressed throughout the year. There are a large number of bulbs (especially lilies) which take up little room and have great flower-power. Lots of plants are scented which is an asset in a small area. Some of the choices are tender and may be damaged or killed in severe cold. They are included because small gardens are often sheltered and have warm micro-climates, so it is worth experimenting to see if you can bring an exotic plant through the winter. Finally, some plants are quite simply big. They can be kept pruned of course, but it is worth remembering that a small garden with only small plants is probably dull and bitty. Large plants have great impact and surprise.

OPPOSITE: Hanging baskets suspended from walls are a way of bringing colour and vitality to even the smallest areas. These weather-tolerant petunias will flower from late spring until late autumn and are trouble free.

10

Be generous with plants. It is not difficult to fill a small space.

HOW TO USE THIS BOOK

Approximate measurements of a plant's height and spread are given in both metric and imperial measures. The height is the first measurement, as in for example 1.2m × 60cm/4 × 2ft. However, both height and spread vary so greatly from garden to garden since they depend on soil, climate, pruning and position (a plant grown in a container may well have its growth restricted), that these measurements are offered as guides only. This is especially true of trees and shrubs where ultimate growth can be unpredictable. Height only is given for climbers and some tall bulbs.

The following symbols are also used:

○	=	the plant thrives in or tolerates full sun.
◐	=	thrives in or tolerates part-shade.
●	=	thrives in or tolerates full shade.
◌	=	prefers well-drained soil.
◑	=	prefers moist soil (the text will state if the plant requires good drainage as well as moist soil, as is often the case).
◆	=	prefers wet soil.
E	=	the plant is evergreen.
LH	=	needs acid soil and is intolerant of lime.
❊❊❊	=	the plant is fully hardy and can survive winters in temperate regions.
❊❊	=	the plant is only frost-hardy, not fully hardy and it is likely it will need shelter and protection during winter in temperate regions.
❊	=	the plant is tender (or half-hardy) and even in mild winter areas it may need protection to survive, or can be grown under glass.

POISONOUS PLANTS

In recent years, concern has been voiced about poisonous plants or plants which can cause allergic reactions if touched. The fact is that many plants are poisonous, some in a particular part, others in all their parts. For the sake of safety, it is always, without exception, essential to assume that no part of a plant should be eaten unless it is known, without any doubt whatsoever, that the plant or its part is edible and that it cannot provoke an allergic reaction in the individual person who samples it. It must also be remembered that some plants can cause severe dermatitis, blistering or an allergic reaction if touched, in some individuals and not in others. It is the responsibility of the individual to take all the above into account.

1.
SHRUBS and TREES

Abutilon megapotamicum

A semi- or fully evergreen frost-hardy shrub with bright green leaves and bell flowers in summer and autumn. These flowers are noticeable for their red calyx and yellow corolla, with protruding purple-red stamens. In cold areas it is usually grown as a wall-shrub, with its stems trained against supports, but it can be grown in a container, given winter shelter.

Height × spread: 2 × 2m/6 × 6ft

Soil: Ordinary fertile well-drained soil.

Position: Can be grown in a sheltered position against a wall or in a tub or pot or trained as a standard.

Care: Provide winter protection. Prune in mid-spring if needed.

◯ ◊ E ❄❄

Acer palmatum var. *dissectum*: Japanese maple

A Japanese maple with divided and finely cut green foliage which provides autumn colour, when it turns red and gold. It is a slow-growing, mound-forming shrub with drooping branches, elegant in shape, as well as foliage. There is also a reddish-purple leafed form called 'Dissectum Atropurpureum' which makes a fiery display in autumn. Young leaves can be killed by late frosts.

Height × spread: 4.5 × 2.4m/15 × 8ft

Soil: Fertile, moist but well-drained soil.

Position: Shade and shelter are essential whether it is grown in open ground or in a pot.

Care: Protect from cold winds and late frosts. Mulch in autumn.

◐ ◖ ❋❋❋

Acer shirasawanum 'Aureum': Golden Japanese maple

A beautiful, slowish-growing yellow-leafed tree with tiny purple-red flowers. The leaves have between 7 and 11 lobes and the colour persists throughout the year, not turning in autumn. The remarkable foliage is liable to be damaged by winds and also by sun-scorch and the tree needs to be placed with care. It makes a bushy specimen.

Height × **spread:** 6 × 6m/20ft × 20ft

Soil: For fertile, moist but well-drained soil.

Position: Shelter and part-shade are important to prevent wind damage or sun scorch. It can also be grown in a pot.

Care: Protect from cold winds and late frosts. Mulch in autumn.

◑ ◊ ❄❄❄

Alyssum spinosum roseum: Spiny alyssum

A dwarf spiny shrublet making a mounded bush with tangled, wiry stems and small, silver-grey leaves and clusters of small, pale pink flowers in summer. It is prettier than the usual type plant which has whitish flowers. It is a desirable rock plant for its distinctive colouring. It is still sometimes found under its old name, *Ptilotrichum*.

Height × spread: 30–45 × 30–45cm/1–1$\frac{1}{2}$ × 1–1$\frac{1}{2}$ft

Soil: Gritty, well-drained and fertile soil is needed.

Position: Well-suited to being grown in a large trough, rock garden or raised bed.

Care: Ensure good drainage and deadhead after flowering.

○ ◊ ❊❊❊

Argyranthemum 'Vancouver'

A half-hardy sub-shrub with finely cut grey-green leaves and a continuous succession of pink anemone-form daisy flowers from late spring to autumn. It forms a bush with a woody base. Other cultivars worth growing are the similar pale pink 'Mary Wootton' and the single yellow 'Jamaica Primrose'. *A.gracile* 'Chelsea Girl' has wire-thin grey-green leaves and single, white rayed flowers, yellow-centred.

Height × spread: 1m × 75cm/3 × 2¹/₂ft

Soil: It needs well-drained reasonably fertile soil.

Position: Grow in sun as a bedding plant or otherwise in a container, as a bush or trained as a standard.

Care: Pinch out the growing shoots to encourage a neatly-shaped bush. In mild areas they may be over-wintered with a mulch.

Aucuba japonica '**Gold Dust**': Spotted laurel

One of the easiest, most tolerant evergreen shrubs which will brighten a gloomy corner. This is a female plant (unlike some of the forms of the spotted laurel) and persistent and glowing red berries will follow small spring flowers of reddish-purple if a male plant is nearby, such as 'Lance Leaf' or 'Crassifolia'. It is very hardy and will grow almost anywhere.

Height × spread: 3 × 2m/10 × 6ft

Soil: For almost any soil, dry or moist, even poor.

Position: Grow in the open ground or in a tub. Use as a hedge or screen if needed.

Care: Prune in spring if size is a problem.

○ ◑ | ◇ | E | ✳✳✳

Azorina vidallii

A frost-tender, evergreen shrub with shiny green leaves presented in rosettes, and pendant pink or white thick bell-flowers with a waisted and fluted outline in late summer. After flowering the stems don't branch and they will need to be cut off after they have died. The cut stems weep a milky sap which dries to look like brown rubber, so take care this doesn't drip on the leaves.

Height × spread: 60 × 60cm/2 × 2ft

Soil: Best in a free-draining soil which retains moisture.

Position: Plant in a container which can be overwintered inside in cold areas, but it can be short-lived. Place in sun with a little mid-day shade if possible.

Care: Cut off the stems after flowering. In frost-free areas, overwinter outside with protection from the wind.

Bupleurum fruticosum: Shrubby hare's ear

A lovely evergreen shrub which is on the borderline of hardiness. Umbels of starry acid yellow flowers appear from mid-summer to early autumn over the dark blue-green leaves. It is excellent in windswept places and is often to be seen in gardens by the sea. The tiny flowers when massed in late summer give a cloud of dull gold to the plant.

Height × spread: 1.2 × 1.2m/4 × 4ft

Soil: It benefits from well-drained soil.

Position: Grow in full sun and near a wall or fence for protection.

Care: Ensure that the plant has winter protection if grown in a tub.

◯ ◌ E ❋❋/❋❋❋

Buxus sempervirens: Box

A variable evergreen shrub with small green or variegated leaves which is commonly used for topiary or hedges. There are numerous forms, some more robust in growth than others. Box is known for its musty smell which is strong in an enclosed space. If planted in a tub in full sun, it must be kept moist to prevent the leaves yellowing.

Height × spread: Up to 4.5 × 4.5m/15 × 15ft

Soil: Suited to well-drained and fertile soil.

Position: Use in a tub or container, or in open ground as a hedge or screen, or as a specimen.

Care: Clip in high summer to shape. When forming topiary, pinch back new shoots.

○ ◑ | ◊ | E | ❄ ❄ ❄

Buxus sempervirens 'Suffruticosa': Dwarf box

A slow-growing and low-growing form of this evergreen shrub which is often planted to form patterns on a patio or as a low edging to a path or bed. As an edging, the small plants are usually put in at intervals of 15–22cm/6–9in apart. When they grow together, they will give a trim appearance to the feature.

Height × spread: 45 × 30cm/1¹/₂ × 1ft

Soil: For well-drained and fertile soil.

Position: Use as a trim low edging or kerb to a patio or bed.

Care: Mulch well after planting in spring. Clip in summer.

○ ◑ | △ | E | ❄ ❄ ❄

A handsome half-hardy evergreen shrub with bottlebrush flowers (stamens) of rich deep red in summer and long, dark green leaves. *C. salignus* is another species with creamy stamens. In cold areas they need greenhouse protection in winter but can be tried outside trained against a warm wall, and battens with fleece put up as a covering in prolonged frost.

Height × spread: 2 × 2m/6 × 6ft

Soil: For neutral to acid fertile soil, moist and well-drained.

Position: For shelter and full sun, whether in a tub or by a wall.

Care: Prune if needed after flowering. Take out damaged growth.

◯ ◑ LH E ❋

Camellia japonica 'Mathotiana Alba'

A beautiful evergreen shrub which needs shelter to protect its white formal-double flowers. It has dark glossy green leaves. 'Alba Simplex' is a fine single-flowered white form with a centre of golden stamens. White flowers are prone to show frost damage, but single-flowered cultivars drop their petals neatly. Cold winds as much as frost damage the early flowers.

Height × spread: Slow-growing to 2 × 2m/6 × 6ft

Soil: For neutral to acid humus-rich soil which is moist but never waterlogged: ericaceous compost in a container.

Position: Plant in borders where it does not get morning sun, or grow in a tub.

Care: Mulch annually with leaf mould or bark. Don't allow to dry out in autumn or the buds may drop.

◐ ◑ E LH ❄❄❄

Camellia × williamsii 'Elsie Jury'

An evergreen shrub with dark green glossy leaves and
glorious pink peony or anenome-form flowers in spring.
As a very general rule, *Camellia × williamsii* cultivars tend
to be more vigorous in growth than those of *C. japonica*,
and more rangy in habit. Also, in general, they drop their
spent flowers more neatly instead of retaining them to age
on the plant.

Height × spread: 2.4 × 2m/8 × 6ft

Soil: For neutral to acid, humus-rich soil which is moist but never
waterlogged: ericaceous compost in a container.

Position: Plant in borders where it does not get morning sun, or grow
in a tub.

Care: Mulch annually with leaf mould or bark. Don't let it dry out in
autumn or the buds may drop.

◐ ◑ E LH ❄❄❄

Camellia × *williamsii* 'Galaxie'

A very showy, short-branched, evergreen shrub massed with pale pink, darker-veined, formal-double flowers in spring, with dark glossy leaves. Because this cultivar is so twiggy, it is very floriferous and it also means it does not grow fast but remains bushy and compact. Less showy cultivars include the single pink 'J. C. Williams' and trumpet-flowered 'Bow Bells'.

Height × spread: 2 × 2m/6 × 6ft

Soil: For neutral to acid humus-rich soil which is moist but never waterlogged: ericaceous compost in a container.

Position: Plant in borders where it does not get morning sun, or grow in a tub.

Care: Mulch annually with leaf mould or bark. Don't let it dry out in autumn or the buds may drop.

◑ ◐ E LH ❋❋❋

One of the finest frost-hardy evergreen shrubs with shiny dark green leathery foliage and scented, yellow-stamened, white flowers produced in early and mid-summer. It is worth a place on the terrace as a specimen plant or can be grown with other shrubs. Provide it with protection against cold, drying wind. 'Ladham's Variety' has large flowers.

Height × spread: 2 × 2m/6 × 6ft

Soil: For well-drained fertile soil with humus, which will not dry out.

Position: Plant it in shelter in full sun. It can be wall-trained or it can also be grown in a large tub.

Care: It needs minimal pruning but if overcrowded an old branch can be cut out occasionally from the base.

| ◯ | ◊ | E | ❋❋ |

Ceanothus 'Autumnal Blue': Californian lilac

A useful evergreen shrub for bringing blue in mid to late summer to the garden. It is hardier than many ceanothus but will still benefit from shelter. Its leaves are bright green and shiny, the flowers carried in heads of showy panicles. *Ceanothus* 'Burkwoodii' is another late-summer flowering shrub. It is more compact than 'Autumnal Blue' and suited to the small garden, but it is frost-tender.

Height × spread: 2.4 × 2m/8 × 6ft

Soil: For fairly fertile moist but well-drained soil. Avoid shallow chalk.

Position: Plant in sun, against a wall where it can be trained flat if needed. Can also be tub grown.

Care: Mulch and prune in spring, shortening side shoots and ends.

○ ◐ E ❋❋❋

Ceanothus 'Blue Mound': Californian lilac

A domed lower-growing, frost-hardy form of this popular evergreen shrub, massed with clusters of bright blue round flowerheads in spring and small glossy dark green leaves. It will form a brilliant mound, the spread of which may need curbing. Like all ceanothus, it will appreciate a mulch in spring, especially as its canopy may prevent rain reaching the roots.

Height × spread: 1.2 × 1.5m/4 × 5ft

Soil: For reasonably fertile, moist but well-drained soil, though not for shallow chalk.

Position: Plant in full sun in a sheltered spot. It is too spreading for a container.

Care: Prune after flowering, cutting out damaged wood, and liquid feed.

○ ◌ E ✸✸

Cestrum 'Newellii'

An evergreen shrub that is not fully hardy and benefits from shelter, by a wall or on a terrace. Rich crimson flowers, tubular in form, hang in showers from summer to autumn. Crimson-purple berries may follow. Another worthwhile cestrum is the willow-leafed jessamine, *C. parqui*, with clusters of acid-green tubular flowers, opening in stars at the end, scented at night.

Height × spread: 3 × 3m/10 × 10ft

Soil: Well-drained soil that is reasonably fertile is necessary.

Position: It can be grown in a container, or planted out in a sheltered spot by a wall.

Care: Protect in winter. Prune if necessary lightly in spring to shape the plant.

◐ ◊ E ❋❋

A showy form of the flowering quince, with rich, glowing, deep pink flowers in spring and dullish green leaves. In a mild spell in late winter a few flowers will often open early. Yellowish fruits often follow the flowers. Other good cultivars include the very spreading 'Crimson and Gold'. 'Moerloosei' is a pink and white form, like apple blossom, of *C. speciosa*.

Height × spread: 1.5 × 2m/5 × 6ft

Soil: For any ordinary reasonably fertile soil.

Position: Wall-train in sun or part-shade, or it can be grown in a tub if space is limited.

Care: Prune after flowering, cutting side shoots to 2 or 3 buds.

○ ◑ | ◊ | ✳✳✳

Chamaecyparis lawsoniana 'Columnaris': Cypress

A very narrow conifer which makes a spire of densely packed evergreen, rich, deep blue-green foliage. It is effective as an accent plant or several can be used to look like pillars. Another slender-growing form of the cypress is 'Wisselii' with blue-tinged foliage. It is fast-growing but more open, less of a neat pillar, than 'Columnaris'.

Height × spread: 10 × 1m/30 × 3ft

Soil: Tolerant of a wide range of soils, which are moist but well-drained.

Position: Plant in full sun or part shade, using its column effect to the full.

Care: No pruning should be needed. In any case don't cut into old wood.

◯ ◑ ◐ | E | ❄❄❄

Choisya 'Aztec Pearl': Mexican orange blossom

A beautiful compact evergreen shrub with finely cut palm-like leaves and masses of starry, white, fragrant flowers in spring and sometimes in autumn too. It is more compact and not as fast-growing as the common Mexican orange blossom and better suited to small gardens. Its foliage is also a more decorative asset where space is limited.

Height × spread: 1.5 × 1.5m/5 × 5ft

Soil: For any reasonably fertile soil that is well-drained.

Position: It makes a beautiful plant in a large tub or it can be grown in shelter in full sun.

Care: If necessary it can be pruned after flowering.

| ◯ | ◊ | E | ✳✳✳ |

Choisya ternata '**Sundance**': Golden Mexican orange blossom

A hardy evergreen shrub with brilliant golden leaves, particularly when young, which will turn yellow-green in half-shade. It does not flower often. As a top foliage plant it will bring the effect of sunlight to any area in a small garden which is in dappled shade. In a cold draughty position the leaves, and even branches, may be damaged.

Height × spread: 2 × 2m/6 × 6ft

Soil: It will grow in any reasonably fertile soil.

Position: Avoid draughty positions. Grow in sun or shade (though see above), in shelter. Can be tub-grown too.

Care: If needed, it can be pruned after flowering.

○ ◑ | ◊ | E | ❄❄❄

Cistus × *cyprius*: Rock rose, sun rose

A frost-hardy shrub with evergreen foliage and white, crimson blotched, yellow-stamened flowers in early to midsummer produced in great abundance though each blossom lasts for only one day before falling. The leaves are sticky and dark green, turning a rather leaden grey-green in winter. The plant has hybrid vigour and will grow quickly to furnish the garden.

Height × spread: 2 × 1.5m/6 × 5ft

Soil: For well-drained soil (though not heavy chalk) which is fairly fertile.

Position: Can be pot-grown or planted in a warm, sheltered spot by the patio or in a bed.

Care: Give winter protection where needed. No pruning except to cut out old, dead stems.

Cistus **'Peggy Sammons'**: Rock rose, sun rose

A lovely frost-hardy shrub with evergreen leaves of downy grey-green and crinkled pink flowers in early to midsummer with golden centres in great profusion. Each of the flowers only lasts for a day when it will fall like tissue paper. As it is not fully hardy, it deserves being planted at the foot of or near a hot wall.

Height × spread: 1 × 1m/3 × 3ft

Soil: All cistus need well-drained soil, which is reasonably fertile. Avoid heavy chalk.

Position: Excellent in a warm, sheltered spot in full sun.

Care: No pruning should be given except to take out dead stems. Protect in winter.

◯ ◌ E ❋❋

Cistus × *pulverulentus* 'Sunset': Rock rose, sun rose

A compact frost-hardy evergreen shrub with grey-green wavy-edged leaves and an abundance of striking hot magenta flowers with golden centres carried in summer. Each flower will last only a day but the succession makes for a long flowering period. As it is not fully hardy it will need to be placed at the foot of a hot wall.

Height × spread: 60cm × 1m/2 × 3ft

Soil: All cistus need well-drained soil, reasonably fertile. Avoid heavy chalk.

Position: Plant in sun and shelter at the foot of a wall or by a patio.

Care: No pruning should be given. Protect in winter, if necessary.

○ △ E ❄❄

Clematis alpina 'Ruby'

A robust, easy, spring-flowering clematis which has small pendant flowers of dusky rose like lanterns and cream anthers, which are displayed as the bell-flowers open. There is often a repeat flush of flowers in late summer if the plant is not pruned, though on a minor scale. Fluffy seed heads follow the flowers. The foliage is finely divided.

Height: Climbing or trailing to 3m/10ft

Soil: For moist soil which is fertile and enriched with humus, yet well-drained.

Position: It can be tied to a wall, grown over a shrub or planted in a large container to cascade down.

Care: Mulch in spring. Prune to shape after flowering.

○ ◑ ● | ◖ | ❄❄❄

Clematis 'Comtesse de Bouchaud'

A vigorous clematis for mid to late summer which is a reliable variety with flowers up to 10cm/4in across of a pearly mauve-pink with soft yellow anthers, and mid-green leaves. Clematis wilt is often a problem with large-flowered hybrids. As a precaution, plant the root ball about 7.5cm/3in below soil level to encourage new shoots.

Height: Climbing to 3m/10ft

Soil: It needs good humus-rich, moist but well-drained soil.

Position: Train on a wall or trellis or pergola or grow in a large container. Always shade the root.

Care: Mulch in late winter and cut back to strong buds 30cm/1ft from the soil surface.

Clematis 'Etoile Violette'

A late-flowering climber which produces a prolific display of violet-blue flowers with contrasting yellow anthers from midsummer to early autumn. The blooms are about 7.5cm/3in across and the leaves are mid-green. It belongs to the group of Viticella clematis, which are vigorous, hardy climbers, flowering on their new wood, so they are pruned in late winter.

Height: Climbing to 4m/13ft

Soil: It needs humus-rich, moist but well-drained soil.

Position: Train on a wall or a trellis or pergola. Always shade the roots.

Care: Mulch in late winter, and cut back hard to strong buds, 30cm/1ft from soil surface.

| ◐ | ◑ | ✳✳✳ |

Clematis florida 'Sieboldii'

A choice, frost-hardy clematis blooming in mid to late summer with cream flowers which have prominent purple stamens at their centre. It is sometimes likened to a passion flower. The leaves may be semi-evergreen. It is a weak-growing species but its glamour makes it worth trying. Plant the root ball 7.5cm/3in below the soil surface as a precaution against the disease wilt.

Height: Climbing or trailing to 2m/6ft

Soil: Grow in humus-rich, moist but well-drained soil.

Position: It needs full sun and shelter whether trained on a wall or grown in a large container. Shade the roots.

Care: Protect and mulch in winter. In early spring prune to strong buds 30cm/1ft from soil surface.

Clematis macropetala 'Markham's Pink'

A very pretty sugar-pink form of an open, bell-flowered clematis which blooms in spring. The species, *C. macropetala*, has blue flowers, deep violet-blue in the form 'Maidwell Hall'. This type of clematis has flowers which have the appearance of being semi-double or double because the interior is full of small petaloid stamens. The flowers are followed by sticky seed-heads.

Height: Climbing or trailing to 3m/10ft

Soil: Easy in most moist, humus-rich but well-drained soils.

Position: Shade the roots. It can be trained on a wall or trellis or grown in a large container.

Care: Mulch in spring. Prune if necessary after flowering.

○ ◐ | ◗ | ❄❄❄

Clematis 'Niobe'

One of the most beautiful clematis with velvet wine-red flowers with gold stamens, up to 15cm/6in across, blooming for a long period in summer. It has mid- to dark green leaves. It remains a lowish-growing hybrid and can be grown in a container with a minimum diameter of 45cm/1$\frac{1}{2}$ft. In dry weather a container-grown clematis should be watered every day.

Height: Climbing or trailing to 2–3m/6–10ft

Soil: It needs good humus-rich, moist but well-drained soil.

Position: Train on a wall or trellis or grow in a large container. Always shade the roots.

Care: Mulch in spring. Prune lightly in earliest spring, removing dead growth.

Convolvulus cneorum

A frost-hardy shrub with silky, silver, evergreen leaves and white, pink-budded flowers from late spring to summer. The fully open bloom shows the yellow centre. It is a beautiful subject for a sheltered position, although a severe winter is likely to kill it. It can be propagated by cuttings and it is worth trying a couple as a precaution.

Height × spread: 60 × 60cm/2 × 2ft

Soil: Good drainage is essential.

Position: It is well suited to a pot, or planted out in a sheltered spot, perhaps at the foot of a wall.

Care: If container-grown, bring under shelter before severe winter weather.

Daphne cneorum 'Eximia': Garland flower

Scented plants are valuable in a small garden and this low-growing evergreen shrub is one of the best. Pink, very fragrant flowers are borne in late spring, deeper, almost crimson in bud, which gives a two-tone effect to the clusters which are abundant. The leaves are small and narrow, of a darkish slightly grey-green. Unfortunately, it can be short-lived.

Height × spread: 20cm × 1m/8in × 3ft

Soil: Well-drained humus-rich soil, which does not dry out.

Position: For front of beds or gravel in sun but the roots must be shaded.

Care: Mulch the plant with compost or gravel to keep the roots cool.

| ◯ | ◐ | E | ❄❄❄ |

Erysimum 'Bowles' Mauve': Perennial wallflower

A quick-growing, evergreen, short-lived shrub with mauve clusters of flowers from late winter to summer and often again in autumn. These flowers, which are produced in racemes, are only lightly scented, if at all, but are so continuous that the plant earns its space in a small garden. The leaves are narrow and of grey-green.

Height × spread: 75 × 60cm/2^1/$_2$ × 2ft

Soil: Good in well-drained neutral or alkaline soil.

Position: Plant in full sun in beds, gravel or by a patio for colour throughout the year.

Care: Dead-head regularly and prune lightly to keep bushy.

| ◐ | ◌ | E | ❋❋❋ |

Euonymus fortunei 'Emerald 'n' Gold'

A showy, hardy, evergreen shrub with gold leaves with a bright green centre. It can be trained as a standard, or grown as a bush. If given a part-shady position in the garden it will give the effect of sunlight, and tolerate dry soil. If grown in sun, it will require the earth to be more moist.

Height × spread: 1 × 1m/3 × 3ft

Soil: For well-drained moderately fertile soil.

Position: It will lighten a part-shaded corner in a small garden or it can be grown in a container.

Care: Prune if necessary in late spring or early summer.

◐ ◑ △ E ❄❄❄

Euonymus fortunei 'Silver Queen'

A hardy evergreen shrub with white margined green leaves, good for brightening a shady corner. It produces tiny clusters of insignificant cream flowers in late spring to summer. If planted against a wall, it will lend itself to use as a climbing plant, so long as it is trained and supported. In this case it will grow taller.

Height × spread: 2.5 × 1.5m/8 × 5ft

Soil: For well-drained, moderately fertile soil.

Position: For borders or against a wall where it may be trained in order to save space.

Care: Prune if necessary in late spring or early summer.

○ ◐ | ◌ | E | ❄❄❄

Euphorbia mellifera: Honey spurge

A splendid frost-hardy evergreen shrub with rich green leaves, with a pale mid-rib, and honey-scented flower clusters in late spring. It makes an exotic-looking addition beside a terrace. It is not fully hardy and requires a sheltered warm site, though if cut down by cold in winter, it is worth waiting to see if it will re-grow again from the base.

Height × spread: 2 × 2m/6 × 6ft

Soil: For light soil that is well drained.

Position: Grow this plant against a wall for shelter and in full sun.

Care: Protect in cold weather. Milky sap from cut stems may irritate skin.

× *Fatshedera lizei*: Tree ivy

A cross between a *Fatsia* (see opposite) and an ivy, this is a sprawling, frost-hardy, evergreen shrub with glossy, fingered leaves and white flowers in autumn. These flowers are borne in panicles with each cluster terminating its stalk. It is good in cities where it will tolerate some pollution and where shelter is easily available.

Height × spread: 2 × 3m/6 × 10ft

Soil: For moist but well-drained fertile soil.

Position: It can be grown in a container or allowed to sprawl by paving. Its stems can also be trained up against a wall.

Care: Give strong support on a wall as the plant is heavy.

○ ◑ ● │ ◐ │ E │ ❄❄

Fatsia japonica

One of the most splendid evergreen shrubs of architectural appearance for the patio. In autumn cream flowers surmount the glossy leaves, followed by black fruits. It is often used as a coastal shrub because it likes the mildness of the climate. Give it a prominent but sheltered position for the sake of its handsome foliage and late flowers.

Height × spread: 1.5 × 2.5m/5 × 8ft

Soil: Moist but well-drained fertile soil.

Position: Ideal as a large shrub beside paving or it can be container-grown. Shelter is necessary for this frost-hardy subject.

Care: Protect against the effect of cold, drying winds.

○ ◑ | ◐ | E | ❈❈

Fuchsia 'Checkerboard'

A tender, vigorous, free-flowering, upright-growing fuchsia with thin, white reflexed sepals below a red tube and with a rich red corolla. It flowers from summer to autumn. It can be grown in a pot which can be stood out in summer and brought back under glass before the onset of frosts. In time it will form a sizeable specimen.

Height × spread: 1m × 75cm/3 × 2¹/₂ft

Soil: For moist but well-drained soil.

Position: Excellent in containers where it will make a bushy specimen.

Care: Give a liquid fertilizer when in growth. Keep dryish in winter.

◖◗ ▲ ❄

Fuchsia 'Dollar Princess'

A sturdy, vigorous, free-branching, double-flowered variety of fuchsia with a purple corolla and cerise sepals. This shrub is almost hardy, and flowers from summer to autumn. There are a large number of other showy fuchsias that are almost hardy. In cold areas they are grown as herbaceous perennials. If top-growth is lost, they can re-grow from the base.

Height × spread: 1m × 45cm/3 × 1 1/2 ft

Soil: For moist but well-drained soil.

Position: Grow in a container or plant in the ground and give winter protection.

Care: Protect in the winter and cut off the dead stems in spring after frosts are past.

Fuchsia 'Dusky Blue'

One of the many splendid pendant cultivars that are suited to hanging baskets, with a very double mauve corolla and pink sepals. It flowers abundantly from summer to autumn. Other suitable cultivars include white and rose 'Gay Parasol' and 'Pink Galore'. There is also the red and pink 'Cross Check' which is excellent for hanging baskets. All are tender.

Height × spread: 30 × 60cm/1 × 2ft

Soil: For well-drained but moist, fertile soil.

Position: Plant in a hanging basket or tall container which is sheltered from drying winds.

Care: Water regularly when growing and fertilize with a balanced fertilizer. Check for whitefly.

× *Halimiocistus wintonensis* 'Merrist Wood Cream'

This evergreen shrub is a hybrid of the *Cistus* and *Halimium* species, with cream, maroon-banded flowers in late spring and early summer, over a mound of grey-green leaves which are white-woolly in youth. It is on the borderline of hardiness, like the ordinary × *H. wintonensis* which is similar except for its white, maroon-zoned flowers.

Height × spread: 60cm × 1m/2 × 3ft

Soil: It needs well-drained light soil which is fertile. Avoid heavy chalk.

Position: Place beside a sheltered wall in full sun or can be container-grown if necessary.

Care: Never transplant. Protect in winter. No pruning except for dead stems.

◯ ◌ E ❋❋/❋❋❋

Hebe cupressoides 'Boughton Dome'

A splendid, evergreen, low-growing, mounded shrub with scale-type leaves giving it the appearance of a conifer. It forms a decorative dome, densely furnished with its cypress-like foliage, but scarcely ever flowering. It is very slow-growing so can be grown in a rock garden or in a container for years before becoming unsuitably large.

Height × spread: 30 × 60cm/1 × 2ft

Soil: Easy in even poor soils, neutral or alkaline.

Position: Suited to being grown among low, carpeting plants like thymes, or among alpines.

Care: Give it some shelter. No need for pruning.

○ ◑ | ◌ | E | ✳✳✳

Hebe 'Pewter Dome'

A handsome, mounded, evergreen shrub with glaucous leaves and a mass of white flowers covering it in summer. It will in time form a sizeable spreading dome, but never loses its shape or neatness. Its foliage provides a dense year-round cover and it is excellent for helping the garden look furnished in winter.

Height × spread: 1 × 1m/3 × 3ft

Soil: Enjoys a well-drained and reasonably fertile, neutral to alkaline soil.

Position: For filling a paving gap near the house for shelter, or for planting near a wall.

Care: As it is not fully hardy, protect in severe winters.

| ○ | ◊ | E | ❋❋ |

Hebe pinguifolia 'Pagei'

A useful, low-growing, evergreen shrub with blue-grey leaves and a snowstorm of tiny white flowers in late spring and early summer. These clusters of flowers held on spikes on the ends of the branches may be repeated later in the year. It is reliably hardy in an open sunny position and will provide dense ground cover.

Height × spread: 30cm × 1m/1 × 3ft

Soil: Easy in most neutral to alkaline soils.

Position: Use as a ground-cover mat beside taller shrubs or in a paving gap, or at the front of a border or raised bed.

Care: Trouble free, and no pruning needed.

◐ ◊ E ❄❄❄

Hebe rakaiensis

A rounded, hardy, evergreen shrub with bright, apple-green leaves and racemes of tiny white flowers in summer. It is excellent in winter when it will help clothe the garden. Its foliage, which provides a dense cover to the plant, is resistant to bad weather, though, as with all evergreens, snow should be brushed off the plant's surface, lest it splays its shape.

Height × spread: 1 × 1.2m/3 × 4ft

Soil: Easy in most neutral to alkaline soils.

Position: Good beside a terrace, or in a gap within paving; or used as an evergreen border plant.

Care: Trouble-free, and no pruning needed.

| ◯ | ◌ | E | ❄❄❄ |

Hedera helix **'Buttercup'**: Ivy

One of the brightest ivies, golden yellow in sunshine, pale green in shade. A good self-clinging evergreen climber on a wall or fence, the mature leaves are large, up to 7.5cm/3in and five-lobed, the young ones near the shoot tips smaller. It is a moderate grower and easily restricted as required. The ivy cultivar, 'Angularis Aurea', is also suffused with yellow.

Height: 2m/6ft

Soil: Not fussy about soil.

Position: Its colour will brighten in sun. If planted in full shade this ivy will lose its distinction and revert to green.

Care: Prune if required in the spring.

| ○ ◑ | ◌ | E | ❄❄❄ |

Hedera helix 'Goldheart': Ivy

The variegated ivies are useful, self-clinging, evergreen climbers to light up part-shaded situations. This has gold-yellow splashes on dark green, leathery leaves. It is a fairly vigorous grower but slow in youth to establish itself. Feeding and mulching will speed it on its way. A cooler appearance is achieved by planting 'Glacier', an ivy with grey-green and silver leaves.

Height: 8m/25ft

Soil: Not fussy about soils.

Position: Its variegation is more pronounced grown as a climber than as ground cover.

Care: Prune if required in the spring.

◐ ◑ | ⬩ | E | ❄❄❄

Helianthemum 'Annabel': Rock rose

A summer-flowering indispensable evergreen shrub for the patio. This is 'Annabel' with semi-double pink flowers (double blooms last longer than single flowers) and grey-green leaves. There are numerous named forms, all blooming for a long period. They are at their most spectacular when massed to form rugs of brilliant colour, though clashes are best avoided.

Height × spread: 20 × 45cm/8in × 1 1/2ft

Soil: For sharply drained soil.

Position: Plant in full sun beside paving or in gaps amongst slabs, or grow in a container or as a front-of-border subject.

Care: Prune them back after flowering to prevent straggliness.

◯ ◌ E ❄❄❄

Helianthemum 'Wisley Primrose': Rock rose

A spreading, grey-green-leafed, evergreen shrub with soft
lemon flowers in summer produced in profusion. Each
flower has a short life, but the succession is so abundant
and continuous that the season of flowering is long.
'Wisley Pink' is a robust pink-flowering form with silvery-
grey leaves. All these single flowers have golden centres.

Height × spread: 25 × 45cm/10in × 1¹/₂ft

Soil: For sharply drained soil.

Position: In full sun, plant beside paving or in paving gaps, or use as
a front-of-border subject.

Care: Prune back after flowering to prevent straggliness.

○ | ◐ | E | ❋❋❋

Helichrysum italicum **subsp.** *serotinum*: Curry plant

Grow this silver-leafed sub-shrub by the house if you like
the curry scent of the foliage. Gold bobble flower-heads
are borne in summer, and these are often cut off before
developing to prevent the effect of the silver, downy
leaves being spoilt. The stems can also be cut and dried
for use as a decoration in winter.

Height × spread: 60 × 75cm/2 × 2^1/$_2$ft

Soil: It tolerates even poor soil, neutral to alkaline.

Position: Grow in shelter and full sun. Good by paving.

Care: Protect against excessive winter wet and severe frost.

| ◖ | ◌ | E | ❄❄ |

Hydrangea macrophylla 'Madame Émile Mouillère'

This white mop-head hydrangea makes a handsome shrub if it can be kept moist. The flowers start white in summer with pink eyes and age to a soft green and pink in autumn. Its leaves are pale to mid-green. The flowers can be cut for the house and are good for drying.

Height × spread: 1 × 1.5m/3 × 5ft

Soil: It needs humus-rich moist soil.

Position: For borders in a shady spot, or plant in a container or pot.

Care: Don't prune until the spring. Mulch annually in the spring.

○ ◑ | ◐ | ❄❄❄

Itea ilicifolia

A graceful evergreen shrub, not fully hardy, with glossy, holly-like green leaves and long greeny-yellow catkins like icicles to 30cm/1ft borne from summer to early autumn. Late-flowering shrubs are at a premium in the garden, especially if they give year-round leaves. Even against a wall it can become damaged in a hard winter.

Height × spread: 3 × 3m/10 × 10ft

Soil: Grow in moist soil that is well-drained and fertile.

Position: Plant in full sun in shelter and wall-train if necessary.

Care: If wall-trained, prune outward facing shoots in early spring.

○ ◐ E ❄❄

Jasminum officinale: Common jasmine

Valued for its fragrant white flowers from summer to early autumn, this vigorous climber is welcome by the house or on a pergola. Not fully hardy, it needs to be placed in full sun and shelter. Pinkish in bud, the flowers are presented in terminal clusters above the dark green, pinnate foliage. There are forms with white- or yellow-marked leaves.

Height: 7m/23ft

Soil: It is best in well-drained but moist and fertile soil.

Position: Grow against a sunny wall where it has shelter.

Care: Prune to shape after flowering. Protect in winter.

◖	◊	❄❄

Juniperus chinensis 'Aurea': Golden Chinese juniper

A slow-growing and very slim column of golden foliage which is aromatic and covered with small purplish-brown cones in the spring. It is one of the most useful golden-leafed conifers for the small garden because of its neat spire-shape. It bears both juvenile and adult foliage at the same time and remains dwarf for a long time.

Height × spread: 8 × 1.2m/26 × 4ft

Soil: It needs well-drained soil which is light, whether sandy or limy.

Position: Grow in full sun, as an accent plant whether simply in the border or in formal pairs or as several columns.

Care: Add grit if needed to the soil to ensure thorough drainage.

| ◯ | ◌ | E | ❋❋❋ |

Juniperus communis 'Hibernica': Irish juniper

A slowish-growing conifer with a thin columnar habit. Its evergreen foliage is very dense and greyish-green. It can be grown as a specimen or an accent plant. Another slim form of juniper is *J. scopulorum* 'Skyrocket' which is narrower and more pointed. These accent plants can be used in garden design like the Italian cypress and are much hardier.

Height × **spread:** 4m × 45cm/13 × 1½ft

Soil: It will tolerate most soils, including chalk or sand, that are well-drained.

Position: Plant in full sun. It is useful in hot, dry places.

Care: Add grit if needed to the soil to ensure good drainage.

○ | ◌ | E | ✳✳✳

Laurus nobilis: Bay laurel

A frost-hardy tree with evergreen, aromatic, pointed, dark green shiny leaves much used in cooking. It is often clipped into decorative balls. The unpruned tree forms a pyramid that will eventually grow large but it is almost always restricted in gardens. Female trees produce glossy black fruits. In severe winter areas, it should be protected, especially if in a container.

Height × spread: 4 × 2m / 13 × 6ft

Soil: It needs well-drained soil that is moist and fairly fertile.

Position: Plant in shelter in sun to protect the young leaves against frost, or grow in containers.

Care: Shape the bush in mid-spring and again in mid to late summer rather than pruning heavily at once.

◐ ◊ E ❋❋

Lavandula angustifolia 'Hidcote': Lavender

One of the neatest small lavenders and among the best. A durable hardy shrub with silver-glaucous, scented, needle-like leaves and rich violet flowers from mid to late summer, noted for their fragrance. The leaves and flower-heads lend themselves to being dried and added to pot-pourri or sachets. It is one of the basic all-purpose plants.

Height × spread: 60 × 45cm/2 × 1¹/₂ft

Soil: Suited to light and fairly fertile soil.

Position: Plant in full sun beside the patio, in paving gaps or in a container, or use as an edging.

Care: Prune routinely in spring as new growth starts. Don't cut into old wood.

○ ◊ E ❋❋❋

Lavandula stoechas: French lavender

A sharply aromatic form of lavender with rich violet, scented flower heads from late spring to summer and evergreen needle leaves of grey-green. It is on the borderline of hardiness. There is a variant of the species called *L.s.* subsp. *pedunculata* with long bracts like rabbit's ears extending well above the flowering spikes. It is a good container plant.

Height × spread: 60 × 60cm/2 × 2ft

Soil: Suited to light and fairly fertile soil.

Position: Plant in full sun by the patio, or in a container, or near a hot wall.

Care: Protect in winter. Prune only lightly in spring and never into old wood.

| ○ | ◊ | E | ❋❋/❋❋❋ |

Lavandula stoechas f. *leucantha*: French lavender

A white-flowered form of the French lavender with pale green, evergreen needle-like leaves. The plant is in flower from late spring to summer and the blooms are scented, leaving their fragrant oil on the hand if rubbed. Like the violet species it is on the borderline of hardiness and needs protection in winter, especially if grown in a container.

Height × spread: 60 × 60cm/2 × 2ft

Soil: Best in light and fairly fertile soil.

Position: Plant in full sun by the patio, or in a container.

Care: Protect in winter. Prune only lightly in spring and never into old wood.

[○] [◐] [E] [❄❄/❄❄❄]

Lavatera maritima: Mallow

A beautiful evergreen shrub that is not fully hardy, with downy grey-green, lobed leaves and soft lavender-pink, rose-centred flowers in abundance from summer to autumn. It is liable to damage in winter, even if not killed, and it is best to check any new growth from low down the stems before attempting to cut out dead parts.

Height × spread: 2 × 2m/6 × 6ft

Soil: Best in light, well-drained soil that is fairly fertile.

Position: Grow in full sun, protected by a wall or in a large container.

Care: Protect in winter, covering the lower parts especially.

| ◯ | ◌ | E | ❄❄ |

Lonicera periclymenum **'Serotina'**: Late Dutch honeysuckle

A vigorous, twining climber which flowers in mid to late summer, producing sweetly scented, creamy-white flowers that are crimson in bud and purple-crimson on the outside. Clusters of bright, glossy red berries follow on from the flowers. The leaves are mid-green. 'Belgica' is the form called Early Dutch Honeysuckle and flowers a little earlier.

Height: 6m/20ft

Soil: It needs fertile, moist, humus-rich soil that is also well-drained.

Position: Grow on a wall or a fence, against a trellis or pergola.

Care: Keep the roots cool with a mulch. Prune after flowering.

Magnolia × loebneri 'Leonard Messel'

A small tree or tall shrub for the small garden with starry
lilac-pink flowers up to 12.5cm/5in wide, produced in
spring on bare branches, the pale green leaves emerging
shortly after. These leaves will remain pale for a long time
deepening slightly as the season advances. It is one of the
most beautiful of the spring-flowering trees for small
gardens.

Height × spread: 8 × 6m/25 × 20ft

Soil: Best in moist but well-drained humus-rich soil. It tolerates some
alkalinity if moist.

Position: Plant in sun or part shade in shelter to protect the spring
flowers from cutting winds.

Care: Mulch the tree well in spring with leaf mould.

○ ◑ | ◊ | ❄❄❄

Magnolia stellata: Star magnolia

An old favourite, with starry white flowers in spring on bare, twiggy branches. There are forms like 'Royal Star' which are worth seeking out for their larger flowers with more petals. 'Centennial' has flowers of the largest size, nearly 15cm/6in across. There is also a dark pink, large-flowered form which is called 'Rubra'.

Height × spread: 3 × 4m/10 × 13ft

Soil: It needs moist but well-drained, humus-rich soil, and tolerates some alkalinity.

Position: Plant in sun or part shade in shelter to protect early spring flowers.

Care: Mulch the shrub well in spring with leaf-mould.

◐ ◑ | ◔ | ✳✳✳

Magnolia 'Susan'

A shrub of upright habit with scented rose-pink goblet flowers, purplish on the reverse, up to 15cm/6in long, carried in spring on the bare branches. Mid-green leaves develop after. It, as well as the cultivar 'Betty', is a hybrid between *M. stellata* and *M. liliflora* 'Nigra', the latter later-flowering with darkest purple-red, goblet-shaped blooms.

Height × spread: 4 × 3m/12 × 10ft

Soil: For moist soil that is enriched with humus yet well-drained.

Position: Plant so that the shrub's flowers are sheltered from cold spring winds.

Care: Mulch the shrub in spring with leaf-mould.

| ○ ◑ | ◔ | ✳✳✳ |

Malus 'Red Sentinel': Crab apple

A small crab apple, upright in habit, with dark green leaves and white flowers in spring followed by a spectacular display of shiny red fruits, gold flushed at first, which usually persist on the tree through winter. It is one of the best small decorative trees in that it produces a show for more than half the year.

Height × spread: 5 × 5m/16 × 16ft

Soil: Grow the tree in well-drained but moist soil which is fairly fertile.

Position: Ideal in a spot where height and shade are needed, and winter colour can be seen from the house.

Care: Mulch in early spring when young. If needed, prune out crowded branches in late winter.

○ ◊ ❄❄❄

Melianthus major: Honey bush

One of the most splendid half-hardy foliage shrubs with blue-green toothed leaves and racemes of brownish-red flowers in late spring to midsummer. In colder regions it may survive winter, behaving as a herbaceous perennial. It is vigorous and even when cut down by frost, it will grow fast annually to be a strong presence with a sub-tropical effect.

Height × spread: 1.2 × 1m/4 × 3ft

Soil: It needs fertile, moist but well-drained soil.

Position: Grow in sun, in a hot sheltered position under a wall, or in large containers if in colder regions.

Care: Plant out in spring after frost. Protect thoroughly in winter.

| ◯ | ◑ | ✳ |

An evergreen shrub of neat form, not completely hardy, not unlike a conifer, with small rich green leaves, golden beneath, and white, very scented flower-heads in early summer, opening from orange buds. The reverse of the small linear leathery leaves and the stems is covered with an inflammable gum, hence its popular name. The white flowers smell of honey.

Height × spread: 1 × 1m/3 × 3ft

Soil: It needs well-drained soil which is fairly fertile.

Position: Plant in sun in shelter by a terrace or a wall.

Care: No especial care but it is worth protecting with fleece in cold winters.

Parahebe cataractae

A very valuable and pretty low evergreen sub-shrub covered in racemes of soft mauve-blue flowers, zoned red with white centres in early summer for a long period. There is also a white-flowered form, similarly zoned. Both types make excellent groundcover underplanting for taller herbaceous plants or for roses, though they are not for very exposed cold positions.

Height × spread: 30 × 45cm/1 × 1^1/₂ft

Soil: Easy in most poor to fairly fertile soils if well-drained.

Position: Plant in shelter in full sun at the front of small beds, in paving gaps and among gravel where it will root along.

Care: Deadhead the spent flower stems to be rewarded with a later flush.

Passiflora caerulea **'Constance Elliott'**: Passion flower

A very vigorous, frost-hardy climber with deep green divided leaves and beautiful, scented white flowers with creamy filaments from summer to autumn. It is a variant of the better-known blue passion flower. Orange oval fruits follow. Other species such as the pink *P. mollissima* or cerise *P. antioquiensis* need cool greenhouse conditions in regions that are prone to frost.

Height: Climbing to 10m/30ft or more.

Soil: It needs well-drained but fairly fertile moist soil.

Position: Plant in full sun in shelter by the terrace or house at the foot of a wall.

Care: Train against a trellis/wall. Protect in winter. In spring prune out dead stems.

Potentilla fruticosa 'Princess'

A neat bushy shrub with delicate pale pink, gold-stamened flowers produced from late spring to mid-autumn in sun. It fades to white in strong sun. Other pretty cultivars of *P. fruticosa*, which is one of the workhorses of the garden, are 'Abbotswood', slightly larger, with blue-green foliage and white flowers. 'Red Ace' has scarlet flowers, which fade in heat.

Height × spread: 60cm × 1m/2 × 3ft

Soil: Easy in almost any soil so long as it is well-drained.

Position: A good floriferous shrub for the front of a bed or border or on the patio.

Care: No special pruning needed. Mulch in spring.

◐ ◊ ✳✳✳

Prunus 'Amanogawa': Oriental cherry

This familiar columnar cherry is often planted in small gardens because it takes little space. It bears an abundance of semi-double, blush pink, scented flowers in mid-spring. Its new leaves are light bronze then green, then turn yellow and red in autumn. Its emphatic shape makes it suitable for specimen planting or two or three trees could be used as accent plants.

Height × spread: 8 × 4m/25 × 12ft

Soil: It needs well-drained but moist and fertile soil.

Position: Plant in full sun. Site it with care because of its shape as a pillar.

Care: Pruning is not needed because of its shape.

| ◯ | ◌ | ❄❄❄ |

Prunus × ***subhirtella*** **'Autumnalis Rosea'**: Winter-flowering cherry

A very valuable small tree for its prolonged flowering period, opening its clusters of semi-double pink flowers in autumn then continuing successfully through winter, to spring for a last burst, normally when the new bronze leaves emerge, turning green. The form which is simply called 'Autumnalis' has pinkish buds which open to white or blush semi-double flowers.

Height × spread: 8 × 8m/25 × 25ft

Soil: It needs well-drained but moist and fertile soil.

Position: Plant in full sun. Lovely with autumn/winter or spring flowering bulbs planted beneath.

Care: Pruning is not desirable, but if needed, do this in summer to avoid the disease of silver leaf.

Pyrus salicifolia 'Pendula': Weeping silver pear

A popular small tree with weeping branches clothed in narrow, willow-like, silver-grey leaves and bearing small creamy flowers in spring. Small green 'pears' follow. It grows fairly fast and can be used as a specimen tree. It was very effectively planted in the white garden at Sissinghurst Castle and is one of the best trees for this colour theme.

Height × spread: 6 × 6m/20 × 20ft

Soil: It enjoys fertile soil that is well-drained.

Position: A good specimen tree that deserves all-round space for its ornamental habit.

Care: No routine pruning. For a dense canopy, prune shoots by one-third in late winter and mid-spring.

Rhododendron leucaspis

A pretty, slightly tender, low-growing shrub with dark green, bristly leaves, yellow-green on the reverse, and rounded, open, white flowers with dark stamens, borne in clusters in late winter or spring. Its small size and branching habit together with its need for shelter makes it suited to being grown in a container which should be protected in winter.

Height × spread: 60cm × 1m/2 × 3ft

Soil: It needs acid, moist but well-drained soil which is rich in leaf-mould: or ericaceous compost in a pot.

Position: Plant at the front of a sheltered part-shady border or in a container which can be protected in winter.

Care: Cut off the spent flowers, mulch each year, protect in winter.

◑ ◐ E LH ❋❋

Rhododendron yakushimanum

This evergreen mounded shrub has given rise to a number of compact popular hybrids. It has dark green leaves, rusty-brown in appearance when young, and rosy buds opening to clusters of pink or white funnel flowers. Some of the many hybrids include 'Seven Stars', soft pink with a purple flush, and the frilly lavender 'Caroline Allbrook'.

Height × spread: 1 × 1.5m/3 × 5ft

Soil: Acid soil is needed which is moist, well-drained and enriched with humus.

Position: Grow the plant in sun or part shade in a bed with other acid-loving plants.

Care: Deadhead the spent flowers and mulch annually with leaf-mould.

Rosa 'Amber Queen': Cluster-flowered rose bush

A compact rose bush, belonging to the group that used to be called Floribunda, with dark green, bronze-tinted, leathery leaves and cupped, fragrant densely petalled flowers of glowing amber. It blooms for a very long period from summer to autumn. If pruning is necessary, this can be done in spring when the shoots can be cut back by one third.

Height × spread: 60 × 60cm/2 × 2ft

Soil: For fertile, moist but well-drained soil.

Position: Excellent for the front of a bed or a border or small enough for a patio.

Care: Feed and mulch in spring, feed in summer and deadhead spent flowers.

Rosa **'Blush Noisette'**: Noisette climbing rose

This was the original Noisette rose and still good, with clusters of prettily cupped, pinky-white flowers, scented of sweet cloves. It blooms very continuously from summer to autumn. It can be grown as a shrub too, though its stems are somewhat relaxed. If grown as a climber, train it on wires. Dead wood should be cut out in winter as needed.

Height × spread: 2.2 × 1.2m/7 × 4ft

Soil: For fertile, moist but well-drained soil.

Position: It can be grown on a sunny wall, trellis, arch or pergola but needs shelter from cold winds.

Care: Feed and mulch in spring, feed in summer and deadhead spent flowers.

Rosa 'Ferdinand Pichard': Hybrid Perpetual rose

For lovers of striped roses this is one of the best with pink and red stripes on pale pink, very scented, double flowers from summer to autumn. It has healthy foliage of light green. It is vigorous and will send out long shoots. To keep it neat, prune the shoots by about one third in spring.

Height × spread: 1.5 × 1.2m/5 × 4ft

Soil: For fertile, moist but well-drained soil.

Position: It is an eye catcher in a sunny bed or border.

Care: Feed and mulch in spring, feed in summer and deadhead spent flowers.

| ◯ | ◊ | ❋❋❋ |

Rosa 'Gentle Touch': Dwarf cluster-flowered bush rose

This miniature rose bears very dainty soft pink, semi-double flowers opening from exquisite buds, continuously from summer to autumn, over dark green leaves. It is a good container plant because it is so floriferous and the delicate buds make it worth specimen treatment. Pruning is normally minimal though the shoots can be reduced in early spring by up to one third.

Height × spread: 45 × 45cm/1½ × 1½ft

Soil: For fertile, moist but well-drained soil.

Position: It can be grown on the patio in a container or at the front of beds.

Care: Feed and mulch in spring and midsummer. Deadhead spent flowers.

◯ ◊ ❋❋❋

Rosa 'Graham Thomas': English rose

A robust modern shrub rose with fully double, large, cupped, golden blooms and bright green healthy foliage. It has an arching habit and blooms from summer to autumn. These English roses are a fairly recent introduction, typically with 'Old Rose' style flowers but with the repeat-flowering capacity of modern bush roses. One of the best cultivars is the fragrant pink 'Heritage'.

Height × spread: 1.2 × 1.2m/4 × 4ft

Soil: For moist but well-drained soil which is rich and fertile.

Position: A valuable rose in a border, well positioned among blue perennials.

Care: Prune stems by one third in late spring. Feed and mulch in spring, feed in summer. Deadhead spent flowers.

96

Rosa **'Nathalie Nypels'**: Dwarf Polyantha rose

Prolific semi-double, bright chalky-pink flowers with lemony stamens are borne on a vigorous but compact bush with healthy dark leaves. They are scented and in continuous bloom from midsummer to autumn, sometimes even into winter. It can be pruned by reducing the shoots by up to one half in early spring and side shoots to two or three buds.

Height × spread: 1 × 1m/3 × 3ft

Soil: For fertile, moist but well-drained soil.

Position: Lovely in a mixed border, by the patio or can be grown in a large pot.

Care: Feed and mulch in spring and feed in midsummer. Deadhead spent flowers.

Rosa 'Sweet Dream': Patio rose

A very neat patio rose with an upright habit of growth and clustered with tidy, full-petalled, peach-apricot flowers with some scent, carried from summer to autumn. It belongs to the group known as dwarf cluster-flowered roses. Its stems and side shoots can be reduced by one third in late winter or early spring.

Height × spread: 38 × 30cm/1ft 3in × 1ft

Soil: For fertile, moist but well-drained soil.

Position: Ideal for the front of a small bed or border, on the patio or for growing in a container.

Care: Feed and mulch in spring. Feed in midsummer. Deadhead spent flowers.

◐ ◊ ❋❋❋

Salix caprea **'Kilmarnock'**: Kilmarnock willow

A notable small weeping willow with yellow shoots and leaves of deep green, greyish on the reverse. Long grey male catkins with yellow stamens are borne on leafless branches in spring. It is one of the neatest, smallest weeping trees, taking up very little space. (Another candidate is *Cotoneaster* 'Hybridus Pendulus' grown as a standard with red berries following white flowers.)

Height × spread: 2 × 2m/6 × 6ft

Soil: The soil for this willow needs to be moist, though well-drained. Avoid shallow chalk.

Position: Plant in full sun and site as a specimen with all-round space.

Care: Mulch in spring. No special pruning needed.

◖ ◊ ❄❄❄

Salvia officinalis **'Purpurascens'**: Purple sage

An indispensable basic sub-shrub for sun with purple-flushed, hairy, grey-green, evergreen leaves and mauve-blue lipped flowers in summer, though it is grown chiefly as a foliage plant. It can be used for cooking purposes. 'Tricolor' is another form of sage with decorative foliage, its grey-green leaves marked yellowish-white and pinkish-purple.

Height × spread: 75 × 75cm/2$^{1}/_{2}$ × 2$^{1}/_{2}$ft

Soil: For well-drained but moist, fairly fertile soils.

Position: Plant in full sun beside paving or amongst colour-toned schemes in beds.

Care: Give the plant shelter and protect from excessive winter wet. Prune lightly if needed in late spring.

◯ ◊ E ❋❋

Santolina pinnata subsp. *neapolitana*

An indispensable patio shrub with needle-thin, grey-green, evergreen aromatic leaves on a plant which forms a low spreading mound. Flower stems rise in summer surmounted by soft, yellow heads (in the form 'Sulphurea') or creamy white ('Edward Bowles'). It can be used to make low hedging, in which case it may be prevented from flowering, which can spoil the shape.

Height × spread: 75cm × 1m/2½ × 3ft

Soil: It will tolerate poor soil (or only fairly fertile) but needs good drainage.

Position: Plant in full sun as an edging shrub, by the patio or use as a low hedge.

Care: Clip over in spring after frosts are past to maintain a neat shape.

◯ ◊ E ❄❄

Sorbus vilmorinii

A dainty, small tree, arching in growth, with leaflets of dark, glaucous foliage, and heads of white flowers in spring which are followed by deep carmine berries in late summer to autumn ageing to pink then white. Other pretty sorbus of the mountain ash kind for the small garden include 'Chinese Lace' with orange-red berries and the yellow-fruited 'Joseph Rock'.

Height × spread: 5 × 5m/15 × 15ft

Soil: It prefers well-drained but moist soil which is neutral to acid.

Position: Plant in full sun or light shade in a small border or use it as a specimen.

Care: Pruning should be minimal. Mulch the tree in spring.

◐◑ △ ❄❄❄

Vinca minor **'Alba Variegata'**: Lesser periwinkle

A useful evergreen sub-shrub which makes prostrate ground cover, with pale green leaves, edged and splashed with gold, and starry white flowers mainly in spring but occasionally later. Other *Vinca minor* cultivars have blue or burgundy flowers. The prettiest of the small carpeting vincas is *V. difformis* with dark glossy leaves and milky-blue, five-petalled flowers, but it is not fully hardy.

Height × spread: 20cm/8in × indefinite spread

Soil: It tolerates a wide range of soils, unless exceedingly dry.

Position: Plant as evergreen ground cover under shrubs or by gravel or paving.

Care: If the plant spreads too invasively, prune it back in spring.

○ ◐ | ◊ | E | ❄❄❄

2.
PERENNIALS, BULBS, ANNUALS and BIENNIALS

Acaena **'Blue Haze'**: New Zealand burr

A very spreading evergreen red-stemmed plant of prostrate growth. It is grown for the attractive blue-grey small, toothed foliage which will make a dense carpet. Red-brown burrs are carried in midsummer which will cling to anything that brushes them. It is extremely vigorous, as are most other acaena, and may be too invasive beside other plants.

Height × spread: 7.5cm × 1m/3in × 3ft

Soil: It will tolerate almost any well-drained soil.

Position: Excellent planted in a hole amongst paving or it will root widely in gravel.

Care: Seedlings or rooted stems may need removing if the plant needs restricting.

○ ◑ △ E ❄❄❄

Adiantum pedatum: Northern maidenhair fern

A fern with delicate green fronds, spraying out on
blackish stems, produced from a slowly spreading
rootstock. It is semi-evergreen or deciduous depending on
conditions, and almost hardy. Like all ferns, it is a
beautiful and useful foil to the shade-loving flowering
plants, or for planting by other choice ferns in sunless
conditions. A similar species is *A. aleuticum*.

Height × spread: 45 × 45cm/1 1/2 × 1 1/2ft

Soil: For moist but well-drained soil, enriched with humus.

Position: Plant in part-shade in a well-sheltered position.

Care: Protect from heavy prolonged frost. The rhizomes can be divided
in early spring if wanted.

◑ ◐ | Semi-E | LH | ❅❅/❅❅❅

Agapanthus **Headbourne Hybrid**: African lily

A stately, frost hardy to hardy deciduous perennial with heads of blue or blue-purple, funnel-shaped flowers in midsummer and rushy green leaves. It is very variable in quality and size, though it is usually sold under this name by nurseries even though it is not uniform. The flowerheads can be used for cutting. If left on the plant they will form handsome seed-heads.

Height × spread: 75 × 75cm/2¹/₂ × 2¹/₂ft

Soil: It tolerates ordinary fertile soil which is moist but well-drained.

Position: It is excellent beside paving, or it can be grown in a pot. Full sun is necessary.

Care: Plant in spring. Deadhead. Remove debris and mulch for protection in winter.

☉ ◊ ❄❄/❄❄❄

Agapanthus 'Lilliput': African blue lily

A handsome small perennial with clusters of funnel-shaped flowers of an intense deep blue in mid to late summer. It is one of the more dwarf forms, suitable for containers. Taller cultivars with rich, deep blue flowers include 'Loch Hope' which grows to 1.5m/5ft and 'Ben Hope', slightly shorter, which is also a good dark blue. 'Blue Giant' is also to be recommended.

Height × spread: 45 × 45cm/1 ¹/₂ × 1 ¹/₂ft

Soil: For moist but well-drained fertile soil.

Position: Plant in full sun whether in the ground or in containers to which it is well suited.

Care: Plant in spring. When container-grown, feed with liquid fertilizer regularly. Deadhead.

| ○ | ◊ | ❋❋❋ |

Ajuga reptans 'Burgundy Glow': Bugle

A quickly spreading evergreen perennial which makes useful ground cover. Among other variegated forms with decorative leaves this one has silver-green leaves with a maroon cast. Spikes of dark blue flowers are borne in spring. Other forms include 'Catlin's Giant' which has ruby-bronze leaves and 'Multicolor' (formerly 'Rainbow') with pink and green splashes on a purple-bronze base. 'Pink Surprise' has pink flowers.

Height × spread: 15 × 60cm/6in × 2ft.

Soil: Easy even in poor soil, but preferably moist.

Position: Grow in sun or part-shade, under shrubs or beside paving.

Care: If it spreads where not wanted take out the excess plants in early summer.

Allium cristophii: Ornamental onion

A stunning hardy bulb with a firework burst of shining mauve stars forming a globe of 20cm/8in across, topping its stem in early summer. Its seedheads are also decorative and can be left to dry on the plant before being taken indoors. The grey-green hairy basal leaves wither before or as the plant is flowering. The plant will self-sow, particularly in suitable conditions like a gravel garden.

Height × spread: 60 × 15cm/2ft × 6in

Soil: Good in most soils provided they are well-drained and reasonably fertile.

Position: Group these bulbs in a sunny border or gravel garden. They also look good with roses.

Care: Plant the bulbs in autumn. In late summer shake the dried seeds where you want them to self-sow.

Allium karataviense: Ornamental onion

A decorative bulb with wide grey-green, velvet, almost horizontal leaves, carrying round heads of starry, pinkish silver-white flowers in summer for a long period. These inflorescences carry about fifty flowers but it is the foliage which adds value to this ornamental onion, lasting for several months. Other decorative onions include the taller globular-headed purple *A. aflatunense*.

Height × spread: 15 × 10cm/6 × 4in

Soil: Well-drained soil that is fairly fertile is essential.

Position: Plant in full sun by paving, in gravelled parts or in raised beds.

Care: Plant the bulbs in autumn which is also the time to detach offsets if wanted.

Anagallis monellii: Blue pimpernel

Gentian-blue flowers with a red eye twinkle on a branching, dwarf, frost-hardy perennial which is grown as a half-hardy annual. It flowers from summer to autumn. For brilliance of colour and its extended period of flowering it can scarcely be equalled in a rock or gravel garden. The small leaves are mid-green and are almost covered by the flowers.

Height × spread: 15 × 30cm/6in × 1ft

Soil: Best in reasonably fertile and well-drained but moist soil.

Position: Plant in full sun for bedding colour or use in a container or raised bed or rock garden.

Care: Sow the seed in spring, planting out after frost. Protect from excessive winter wet, if trying to over-winter.

Androsace lanuginosa: Rock jasmine

A charming silver-leafed trailing perennial with heads of blush, dark-eyed flowers from midsummer onwards. Some forms have a lilac-pink flower. In suitable conditions, where drainage is good or the plant can drape itself over the rocks, the carpet of silver-green rosettes will spread and form a large mat. It is especially valuable for its late period of bloom.

Height × spread: 5 × 60cm/2in × 2ft

Soil: For gritty soil which is well-drained but does not dry out.

Position: Ideally suited to a gravel garden above the edge of a low wall or over the wall of a raised patio.

Care: Take off any dead runners or rosettes and watch for any rotting from wet.

| ◐ | ◌ | Semi-E | ❋❋❋ |

Anemone blanda: Windflower

A quickly spreading little bulb with rayed flowers in early spring of blue, violet, pink, deep rose in the form 'Radar' or white in the form 'White Splendour'. The foliage is composed of dark green leaflets, forming little rugs below the flowers. Other good dwarf anemones include the blue or white *A. apennina* and named forms, lavender blue or white of *A. nemorosa*.

Height × spread: 10 × 10cm/4 × 4in

Soil: It will spread most vigorously in light soil but also enjoys soil that has some humus.

Position: Plant the corms in a border with shrubs or herbaceous plants and allow to naturalize.

Care: Plant in autumn checking carefully that the knobbly tubers are the right way up.

Antirrhinum **(Dwarf bedding)**: Snapdragon

The most useful form of snapdragon for a small garden are the dwarf varieties: short-lived, half-hardy perennials grown as half-hardy annuals. They come in a range of shades – crimson, pink, white, yellow, orange and purple, some of which are bi-coloured. They flower all summer to autumn, forming bushy, branching plants. Look out for rust-resistant cultivars like the Tahiti series.

Height × spread: 20 × 30cm/8in × 1ft

Soil: Well-drained soil that is fertile is needed.

Position: Use these in containers, as edging plants and as front-of-border fillers.

Care: Sow seed in early spring. Deadhead after flowering begins.

| ◯ | ◇ | ❋ |

Aquilegia vulgaris 'Nora Barlow': Granny's bonnet

A sturdy self-supporting perennial with greyish-green segmented leaves and strong stems with very double pompon pale green and deep rose flowers which open from a green double button in late spring and early summer. Other forms of *A. vulgaris* have single or double flowers of violet, blue, white, pink or red. Other excellent aquilegias include the long-spurred McKana hybrids and the Mrs Scott Elliot hybrids.

Height × spread: 75 × 45cm/2¹/₂ × 1¹/₂ft

Soil: For moist but well-drained soil which is fairly fertile.

Position: Plant in sun or part-shade in a border.

Care: If they self-seed, lift where necessary and transfer the seedlings when young as they dislike disturbance.

Arabis ferdinandi-coburgi **'Old Gold'**: Rock cress

A striking evergreen perennial with golden-leafed rosettes.
It is grown for its foliage but also produces small white
flowers in late spring. There is also a variegated form more
commonly available called *A. f-c.* 'Variegata' with green-
and-white-margined leaves. Rock cress which are grown
for their showy flowers rather than foliage include *A.
blepharophylla* 'Spring Charm' with rich purplish-pink
flower heads in spring.

Height × spread: 7.5 × 30cm/3in × 1ft

Soil: It tolerates any ordinary well-drained soil.

Position: It needs an open spot in full sun and is well suited as an
edge to paving or as a low front-of-border plant.

Care: Any stems on variegated forms that revert to green should be
removed.

[○] [◐] [E] [❉❉❉]

Armeria maritima: Thrift

Little pin-cushion flowers in pink, white or purple-red are produced in late spring or summer like small drumsticks above spreading, grassy, evergreen mounds forming cushions of foliage. Various named forms are commonly cultivated including 'Vindictive' which has rosy flower heads and 'Bloodstone', a dark red. 'Alba' is the white form and is excellent as a neat edging. All will make satisfactory ground cover.

Height × **spread:** 20 × 30cm/8in × 1ft

Soil: Easy in ordinary well-drained soil.

Position: A good plant in sun for an open spot by paving, or used for edging.

Care: Deadhead. Increase them by dividing clumps in spring.

| ○ | ◊ | E | ❊❊❊ |

Artemisia alba 'Canescens'

A fine silver perennial with filigree leaves like curled wires. In late summer, spikes of tiny fawn flowers are produced, better cut off as they detract from the effect of the foliage. *Artemisia* 'Powis Castle' is an even more beautiful woody perennial with clouds of feathery silver leaves but it is not fully hardy. It is worth growing in shelter.

Height × spread: 45 × 60cm/1 1/2 × 2ft

Soil: Give the plant well-drained soil which is fairly fertile.

Position: Grow in full sun in the front of a bed or in paving or gravel.

Care: In time it will become woody so prune hard in late summer or spring.

| ◑ | ◌ | Semi-E | ❄❄❄ |

Artemisia schmidtiana 'Nana'

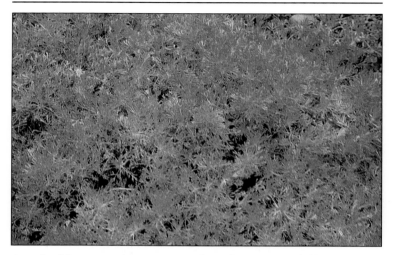

A valuable carpeting perennial with semi- or fully evergreen needle-like leaves of glistening silver. Small creamy-yellow flowerheads are produced in summer, better cut off to encourage foliage. Silver carpets of this kind are an excellent foil to pink or violet flowered bulbs such as the ornamental onions (*Allium*). To achieve the greatest silver effect, grow in a group together.

Height × spread: 5 × 30cm/2in × 1ft

Soil: Well-drained soil which is fairly fertile is necessary.

Position: Grow in full sun, amongst paving or in a raised bed or front of border.

Care: It can be short-lived. To prevent woodiness, clip back in autumn.

| ◯ | ◇ | Semi-E | ❄❄❄ |

Aubrieta hybrids

These are indispensable, evergreen, carpeting and trailing plants for sheets of colour in early spring. There are single or double forms in shades of pink, violet or reddish-purple. There are forms with silver- or gold-margined leaves such as the cultivars 'Argenteovariegata' or 'Aureovariegata'. One of the best semi-double forms is the rich violet 'Greencourt Purple'.

Height × spread: 5 × 60cm/2in × 2ft

Soil: Fertile soil which is well-drained is necessary. Avoid acid soil.

Position: Place in full sun, trailing on a wall or raised bed, or in paving.

Care: Prune after flowering is over to prevent straggliness.

◯ ◌ E ❄❄❄

Begonia × *tuberhybrida*

A variable, frost-tender, tuberous begonia with succulent stems and shiny or dark green leaves. Double or single flowers of white, pink, yellow, orange or red are produced in summer. Plant the tubers in spring in moist compost at 19°C/65°F and pot on, planting out after frost. Lift the tubers in autumn before frosts and overwinter in peat/sand.

Height × spread: 60 × 45cm/2 × 1½ft

Soil: For well-drained humus-rich soil.

Position: Most commonly used in hanging baskets, pots or window boxes but also valuable as bedding plants.

Care: Water well when in full growth, lightly after flowering is over.

Bellis perennis: Daisy

A slow, creeping perennial with quantities of pink, white or red double daisy flowers from spring to summer. It is usually grown as a biennial and is either discarded after its long flowering season, or it can be divided. There are different forms. The Pomponette series is uniformly very low-growing with masses of large, double pink, white or red flowers.

Height × spread: 5–20 × 10–20cm/2–8 × 4–8in

Soil: Easy in any ordinary, well-drained fairly fertile soil.

Position: A charming plant grown as a biennial in troughs or containers or as a bedding plant.

Care: Deadhead the plant regularly to prevent self-seeding.

◐◑ ◊ ❄❄❄

123

Bergenia **'Ballawley Hybrid'**: Elephant's ears

One of the most useful hardy perennials grown for its architectural evergreen leaves which bronze in winter and its crimson flowers in spring. Other excellent forms include the robust 'Bressingham White' and the slightly pinkish-white 'Silberlicht'. The common *Bergenia cordifolia* can be raised easily from seed, which is a cheap way of massing this plant for ground cover.

Height × spread: 60 × 60cm/2 × 2ft

Soil: For any soil with some humus that is not too dry.

Position: Plant in beds or beside paving, in part shade, or sun, though it does not thrive in heat or drought.

Care: Deadhead. Divide congested clumps in spring or autumn and replant.

Callistephus chinensis: China aster

The most useful asters for a small garden are the dwarf cultivars represented here by a rose-red and white example of the Milady series. The daisy flowers of asters come in white, yellow, pink, violet, indigo and bi-colours, borne from late summer to autumn. They are usually grown as half-hardy annuals and as bedding or container plants.

Height × spread: 20–75 × 20–75cm/8in–2$\frac{1}{2}$ft × 8in–2$\frac{1}{2}$ft

Soil: For fertile moist but well-drained soil, though not acid.

Position: Plant out in sun in a sheltered position, in containers or as bedding plants.

Care: Sow the seed in early spring, or after frosts in situ. Stake taller cultivars.

Campanula 'Birch Hybrid'

An invaluable robust perennial (a cross between *C. portenschlagiana* and *C. poscharskyana*) running underground. It has small green leaves and sheets of purplish-blue bells in summer for a very long period. It can be used in a container but it spreads so rapidly that it will need to be frequently divided. It makes a mat of rich bright colour and has become very popular.

Height × spread: 10 × 60cm/4in × 2ft

Soil: For well-drained soil that retains some moisture.

Position: Plant at the front of a bed or beside a paved surface over which it will spread.

Care: Trim if needed after flowering. Rooted stems can be detached to make new plants.

◯◑ ◊ E ❄❄❄

Campanula carpatica 'Blue Clips'

A low-growing perennial which is one of the longest-flowering campanulas with small green leaves covered by a mass of upturned blue saucer flowers (or purple or white in other forms) for a prolonged summer period. It is both showy and easy, putting up with most conditions so long as it isn't waterlogged. Good forms include 'Bressingham White' and 'Jewel'.

Height × spread: 20 × 30cm/8in × 1ft

Soil: For well-drained soil that retains some moisture.

Position: Plant at the front of a border, or within or by a patio, or use as a container subject.

Care: Deadhead as the flowers fade to encourage a fresh burst. Transplant self-sown seedlings as wanted.

Campanula cochleariifolia: Fairy's thimble

This perennial forms a pretty creeping mat of small pale blue or white, single or double nodding bell-flowers in summer. It spreads by running rhizomes and this means it will roam everywhere (as well as seed) including the crevices of paving. There is a white form called 'Hallii'. 'Elizabeth Oliver' is a very dainty soft lavender-blue, double-flowered form.

Height × spread: 10 × 60cm/4in × 2ft

Soil: Best in well-drained but moist soil, neutral or with some lime.

Position: Plant in paving, gravel, a rock garden or in a raised bed. The double forms are good in troughs.

Care: Allow for it to spread, otherwise divide it in spring and replant the rosettes.

Campanula medium: Canterbury bells

The old-fashioned cottage garden plant with bell-shaped pink, white or blue flowers, some forms with a cup-and-saucer effect. It is more usually grown as a biennial in which case it flowers in late spring. Some dwarf forms are grown as annuals and will flower in summer. 'Bells of Holland' comes in this category, with white, pink, lavender or blue flowers.

Height × spread: 45cm–1m × 30cm/1¹/₂–3ft × 1ft

Soil: For fertile moist but well-drained soil, neutral or with some lime content.

Position: Grow in borders in part-shade or full sun. They also make lovely container plants.

Care: Sow seed of biennials in early summer, plant out in autumn. Sow annuals early in the year.

◐◑ ◊ ❋❋❋

129

Campanula poscharskyana

A robust, spreading perennial with mid-green, toothed small leaves and lavender-blue starry flowers in mid and late summer. It will throw out long, flowering stems which will climb by hoisting themselves over neighbouring plants, even the trunk of a tree. Another recommended vigorous dwarf campanula is *C. portenschlagiana* with rich blue-purple bell flowers forming a spreading mound.

Height × spread: 15 × 60cm/6in × 2ft

Soil: It will grow in almost any reasonably fertile soil, even in difficult places.

Position: Excellent in gaps amongst paving, on a wall, a bank or planted as a carpet to a shrub.

Care: Cut back the dead stems after flowering. Watch against excessive spreading.

Cerinthe major 'Purpurascens': Honeywort

A half-hardy, self-seeding annual with grey-green fleshy leaves and stems, and curious navy bracts with grey and purple drooping little bell flowers in summer. It looks appropriate amongst plants which have purple or silvery foliage (like *Artemisia*). Although rather tender, it will self-seed into open spaces such as gaps in paving or gravel and may survive a mild winter.

Height × spread: 45 × 30cm/1¹/₂ × 1ft

Soil: Any well-drained reasonably open soil.

Position: Grow it in a container in full sun or plant out by a patio.

Care: If container-grown, bring the pot of seedlings inside before frosts to overwinter indoors in cold regions.

Chiastophyllum oppositifolium: Lamb's tail

An evergreen perennial forming a carpet of fleshy leaves from which arching spikes with tiny yellow, pendant flowers rise in spring. Coming from Russia it is very hardy and will endure an exposed position, though prefers a shady, moist spot. It will creep along crevices in paving gaps, so can be used to furnish a patio outside traffic areas.

Height × spread: 20 × 30cm/8in × 1ft

Soil: Easy in almost any soil that is moist but well-drained.

Position: Grow in the front of shady beds, in crevices or in a rock garden, or in containers though it is vigorous.

Care: Cut off spent flowering stems. Divide if spreading too rapidly.

◐ ● | ◊ | E | ❈❈❈

Chrysanthemum carinatum 'Court Jesters Mixed'

A very quick-growing annual with rayed flowers of white, red, pink, yellow and orange, zoned with bands of red and orange, and a purple central disc, produced abundantly in summer to early autumn. The divided foliage is smooth and fleshy. This strain was bred especially for amateurs who have small gardens. The flowers can be used for cutting too.

Height × spread: 60 × 30cm/2 × 1ft

Soil: It is easy in most soils, and enjoys good drainage.

Position: A good filler in spaces in beds or borders, giving colour but not taking up too much room.

Care: Sow the seed in spring to early summer where it is to grow.

Clarkia amoena (syn. *Godetia*): Satin flower

A showy hardy annual with single or double flowers of
pink, lilac or cerise, often striped, giving a mass of colour
in summer. There are many different cultivars among this
large group of flowers. One of the best forms for containers
is the Azalea-flowered section which is about 30cm/1ft
tall with semi-double blossom. It is excellent in windy
gardens.

Height × spread: 30–60 × 30cm/1–2 × 1ft

Soil: Any reasonably fertile, moist but well-drained soil, preferably not
limy.

Position: Very good for giving quick colour to a new garden, filling in
gaps in paving or in an annual border.

Care: Sow seed in autumn or winter. Don't transplant.

○ ◑ | ◊ | ❄❄❄

Convolvulus sabatius

A frost-hardy perennial with blue saucer-flowers for a long while in summer, on trailing stems. It will form a woody base and if it is given a sheltered spot and survives winters, it will spread quite widely. It is commonly grown as a container plant from which it will trail. *C. althaeoides* is a similar but pink species.

Height × spread: 15 × 60cm/6in × 2ft

Soil: Fairly poor soil is tolerated but it must be well-drained.

Position: Good as a trailer in a pot or planted in a sheltered, sunny spot at the edge of a raised bed.

Care: Plant in spring. Cut off dead/damaged stems annually.

◐ ◊ ❉❉

Crassula sarcocaulis

A very useful frost-hardy succulent perennial for a late summer display with tiny starry pink or white flowers. It forms the shape of a miniature bush. Its fleshy stems are brittle and liable to break at the joints if knocked, but if they are pushed into earth elsewhere, they will root quickly. Best, though, not to grow it in an exposed position.

Height × spread: 30 × 30cm/1 × 1ft

Soil: It can be grown in poor but well-drained soil.

Position: It needs full sun and is good in gaps in paved areas.

Care: Grow in a warm sheltered position away from traffic areas.

◯ ◌ E ❋❋

Crocosmia 'Lucifer': Montbretia

This is a vigorous perennial with ribbed green, sword-shaped leaves and horizontally held spikes of rich scarlet flowers in mid or late summer. Like the other montbretias, it is valuable for its season of flowering. Other excellent cultivars include 'Solfatare' which is a peachy-yellow, 'Vulcan' which is a rich red and 'Severn Sunrise', apricot-coral and vigorous.

Height × spread: 1m × 7.5cm/3ft × 3in

Soil: It needs moist but well-drained soil, enriched with humus.

Position: Plant the corms in a sheltered spot in a border in clumps which have room to spread.

Care: Mulch in winter. Divide in spring if becoming congested. Deadhead.

○ ◊ ✳✳

Crocus chrysanthus 'Cream Beauty'

A lovely late-winter to early-spring-flowering bulb with cream cups, with gold throats. It has dwarf very narrow linear leaves which should be allowed to die down naturally after flowering. It belongs to a very useful group of early bulbs which are easy and hardy. 'Prins Claus' is another cultivar with white flowers and a purple reverse.

Height × spread: 7.5 × 5cm/3 × 2in

Soil: It is unfussy about soil though good drainage is necessary.

Position: Grow amongst deciduous shrubs at the edge of a bed or in clumps in a border. It can also be grown in a pot.

Care: Plant the bulbs in autumn. Let leaves die down after flowering.

Cyclamen hederifolium

A lovely hardy little bulb which will self-sow and spread
with pink flowers (white in the form of *C.h.* f. *album*) with
reflexed petals in late summer and autumn before the
leaves start. The marbled foliage develops fully later and
lasts from winter to spring before dying down. The tubers
should be planted shallowly. Check that the upper surface
producing the knobbly growth is indeed uppermost.

Height × spread: 15 × 15cm/6 × 6in

Soil: For well-drained soil that has some humus.

Position: Plant under a deciduous tree or shrub in dappled shade.

Care: Mulch well with leaf mould as the leaves die.

◐ ◊ ❋❋❋

Dianthus 'Doris': Pink

A great favourite with its long succession of pale salmon pink double flowers, zoned with a deeper colour, in summer, and neat blue-grey foliage. It belongs to a group of pinks referred to as *D.x allwoodi* varieties, modern hybrids which are very hardy, quick-growing and perpetually in flower. They can be short-lived. 'Doris' is good for cutting.

Height × spread: 30 × 30cm/1 × 1ft

Soil: For neutral to alkaline soil which is well-drained.

Position: It enjoys full sun and a group will provide a long lasting show beside a patio, or at the front of a bed or border.

Care: Plant in spring. Deadhead. Protect from excessive winter wet.

○ ◊ E ❄❄❄

Dianthus gratianopolitanus: Cheddar pink

A useful pretty pink which makes a reliably perennial mat of blue-grey needle leaves, covered with single, very scented, toothed deep pink flowers in summer. It is one of the best and easiest species, still to be found growing in the wild. It is easy to raise from seed sown in the summer and transplanted to a permanent position.

Height × spread: 15 × 30cm/6in × 1ft

Soil: Best in light, well-drained soil which is neutral or has some lime content.

Position: Plant in full sun. Lovely in paving gaps on the terrace, or gravel.

Care: Deadhead the plants after flowering. Tease out debris in winter.

| ◯ | ◌ | E | ❄❄❄ |

Dianthus **'Gravetye Gem'**: Pink

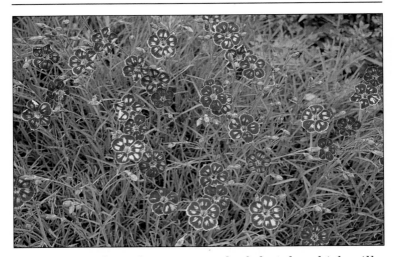

One of the cushion-forming, grey-leafed pinks which will spread into a reliably perennial mat, smothered in clove-sweet crimson and white flowers in summer. Other fragrant small pinks with ruby and white-marked petals include the old cultivar 'Sops-in-Wine' and also 'Waithman Beauty', both slightly taller varieties, not so cushion-forming.

Height × spread: 15 × 30cm/6in × 1ft

Soil: For neutral to alkaline soil that is well-drained.

Position: For front of beds, in gravel, in gaps in paving and in raised beds.

Care: Deadhead the plants after flowering. Tease out debris in winter.

◯ ◊ E ❄❄❄

Diascia rigescens

A sprawling perennial with a profusion of rich salmon-pink flowers in summer, often two heavy flushes, carried in racemes and with small, dull green leaves, which are toothed. It is not fully hardy and liable to be killed in a severe winter. It is best planted in spring after frosts are past and given a sheltered spot.

Height × spread: 30 × 60cm/1 × 2ft

Soil: For reasonably fertile and moist but well-drained soil.

Position: Plant in full sun where it has room to fall forward at the edge of a bed, or in a gap amongst paving.

Care: Deadhead continuously and water during drought. Mulch in winter.

Diascia vigilis

A fairly hardy vigorous species with pretty, pink, spurred flowers all summer to autumn, and a suckering habit. The blossom is carried in racemes and each flower bears markings of deeper crimson and yellow in its central opening. It carries a prolific number of these flowers, and makes a very worthwhile pot plant on a terrace, or planted in a paving gap.

Height × spread: 30 × 60cm/1 × 2ft

Soil: It needs reasonably fertile and moist but well-drained soil.

Position: A charming subject for a container or the front of a bed in full sun, planted where it can spread.

Care: Deadhead continuously, water in drought. Protect in winter.

○ ◖ ❅❅/❅❅❅

Dicentra cucullaria: Dutchman's breeches

A fascinating small perennial with finely cut grey-green leaves and waxy sprigs of white flowers like butterflies in spring. The leaves die down after flowering in spring. Part-shade is suitable and it can be managed easily in a container where it should be allowed to stay almost dry during its summer rest.

Height × spread: 20 × 25cm/8 × 10in

Soil: For humus-rich soil, neutral to alkaline, and gritty.

Position: Plant in a container or in the rain shadow of a wall at the front of a bed.

Care: Allow to die down and keep dry in summer.

◐ ◊ ❄❄❄

Dicentra 'Stuart Boothman'

A spreading perennial, but special for its mound of very blue-grey filigree leaves, with stems of waisted pendant rose bell-flowers in spring to summer. It is one of the best dicentra to plant as a companion to pink or white tulips. Other good dicentra include 'Langtrees' with grey leaves and pinkish-white flowers and 'Luxuriant' with green leaves and red flowers.

Height × spread: 30 × 60cm/1 × 2ft

Soil: Easy in fertile, moist soil enriched with humus, neutral or slightly alkaline.

Position: Plant in part-shade where it can spread at the front of a bed.

Care: Deadhead. If it spreads too widely, divide with care in early spring.

◐ ◌ ❄❄❄

Dierama dracomontanum: Angel's fishing-rod

A graceful small-growing form of the wandflower with rushy leaves growing from corms, and bell-shaped pink or red flowers on arching stems in summer. It is not fully hardy. It will build into clumps of grey-green leaves which are evergreen. The plant will gently self-seed in suitable conditions. Seedlings should be transplanted when young.

Height × spread: 60 × 30cm/2 × 1ft

Soil: It needs well-drained but moist soil which is enriched with humus.

Position: For the front of a border, beside paving or beside a pond.

Care: Plant in spring, water in summer and mulch or protect in winter. Cut off seed-heads if seedlings not wanted.

Dierama pulcherrimum: Angel's fishing-rod

This is a larger form of wandflower with bell flowers on arching stems in summer, variably pink to burgundy. The form shown is called 'Blackbird'. Evergreen rushy leaves grow in tufts from the corms, and it will form sizeable clumps. It dislikes disturbance. It will lightly self-seed. Seedlings should be transplanted when young for growing on.

Height × spread: 1–2m × 60cm/3–6 × 2ft

Soil: Give it moist but well-drained soil, rich in humus.

Position: Plant as a specimen or beside a small pond.

Care: Plant in spring, water in summer, mulch or protect in winter. Cut off seed-heads if seedlings not wanted.

◐ ◑ E ❄❄

Dorotheanthus bellidiformis: Ice plant, Livingstone daisy

Here is a cheerful half-hardy annual with masses of daisy flowers in a wide colour range all summer and succulent pale green leaves. It is more widely known under its former name of *Mesembryanthemum*. The flowers are yellow, mauve, pink, crimson, orange-gold or white, sometimes with bands of another colour. They open fully only in strong sunlight.

Height × spread: 10 × 30cm/4in × 1ft

Soil: It will grow in light, well-drained, even poor soil.

Position: Full sun is essential and it will fill spaces in paving, or gravel.

Care: Sow seed early in the year. Deadhead after flowering has begun.

◑	◊	❄

Epimedium grandiflorum: Barrenwort

A valuable perennial for its spurred spring flowers in white, pink, crimson or yellow. The cultivar shown is 'White Queen' with heart-shaped leaves, suffused with bronze in youth. 'Rose Queen' is equally beautiful with crimson-pink flowers and deep purple-bronze leaves in youth. Both are deciduous. Evergreen epimediums include *E. perralderianum* with glossy, dark green leaves and yellow flowers.

Height × spread: 30 × 30cm/1 × 1ft

Soil: It needs well-drained but moist soil enriched with humus.

Position: Plant in part-shade with shelter for its early flowers.

Care: Deadhead. Remove dead leaves after dying down. Mulch in winter.

Erinus alpinus: Fairy foxglove

An accommodating little perennial, self-sowing, with clusters of pink, purple or white flowers in late spring to summer. The leaves are small, sticky and greyish green, and the plant grows in dwarf tufted clumps. It is fairly short-lived but it will self-sow. There are named varieties, such as 'Dr Hähnle', carmine, and the white *E.a.* var. *albus*.

Height × spread: *7.5 × 10cm/3 × 4in*

Soil: Light, well-drained soil is preferable.

Position: It will grow in cracks in paving or steps, or in gravel.

Care: Deadhead flowers if you don't want them to self-sow.

◖◑ ◊ Semi-E ✻✻✻

Erysimum cheiri: Wallflower

Still a great favourite for bedding and containers, the very fragrant biennial wallflower produces its spring flowers over a long period. Blood-red, cream, yellow, orange, purple and more gentle shades are all available, the latter mostly in the form called Fair Lady Series. Other forms that are true from seed are 'Blood Red' and the Bedder Series.

Height × spread: 20–45 × 30cm/8in–1½ × 1ft

Soil: Good in well-drained neutral or alkaline soil.

Position: Plant as bedding plants, or use in pots, tubs or boxes, especially with tulips.

Care: Sow in early summer and transplant in autumn.

○ ◊ ❋❋❋

Eschscholzia: California poppy

A quick-blooming, hardy annual with finely cut blue-green leaves and a continuous profusion of dazzling poppy flowers, single or double, from summer to autumn in shades of orange or white, yellow, pink or mauve. The Thai Silk Series is low-growing with silken, fluted, semi-double flowers of pink, red or orange. It is useful for cutting.

Height × spread: 15–30 × 15cm/6in–1ft × 6in

Soil: Poor well-drained soil is suitable.

Position: Use for filling gaps in paving or the front of borders. It can also be grown as a container plant.

Care: Sow in situ in spring or autumn.

◖ ◌ ✳✳✳

A choice, low-growing spurge with trailing or prostrate stems with succulent, glaucous, evergreen leaves and yellow flower clusters in spring which are long-lasting. These flower clusters are actually bracts. It will self-sow lightly in suitably gritty soil and the seedlings should be transplanted to a suitable place when young. It is fairly hardy.

Height × spread: 10 × 30cm/4in × 1ft

Soil: It needs very well-drained soil, appreciating grit.

Position: Plant at the front of small beds or raised beds, at the top of walls or in gravel.

Care: If you take cuttings to increase stock, dip them in warm water or charcoal to stop the milky sap bleeding.

◯ ◌ E ❄❄❄

Euphorbia nicaeensis

A hardy evergreen or semi-evergreen perennial with
rosettes of blue-grey leaves and acid-yellow flowerheads
from mid-spring to midsummer. Developing from a woody
roostock, it forms a mound which is a good foil to crimson
or purple flowers in a bed. Other good, evergreen,
perennial euphorbias include *E. rigida* with fleshy grey-
green pointed leaves.

Height × spread: 60 × 45cm/2 × 1¹/₂ft

Soil: For well-drained moderately fertile soil.

Position: Handsome as a permanent planting in paving gaps or
beside the terrace or in a raised bed.

Care: Ensure good drainage. Deadhead and remove dead stems.

◯ ◊ E/Semi-E ❄❄❄

This plant is usually grown as a half-hardy annual (though strictly a sub-shrub) with twinkling blue daisies with yellow centres summer and autumn, and narrow green hairy leaves. If it can be over-wintered under frost-free conditions it can be potted up in spring and will form a sturdy and sizeable bush of 60cm/2ft.

Height × spread: 20 × 20cm/8 × 8in

Soil: For well-drained fairly fertile soil.

Position: Grow in full sun in a container or use as a bedding plant at the front of a border.

Care: Sow the seed in spring, planting out after frosts are past.

◯ ◌ ❄

An imposing bulb for a small garden, with a foxy scent but worth inclusion. Orange-red or yellow flower bells with an interior ring of dark spots, topped with a leaf rosette, are borne on stout stems with light green leaves. The bulbs are dormant by midsummer so it is sensible to mark their position to prevent disturbance.

Height × spread: 1–1.2m × 30cm/3–4 × 1ft

Soil: Well drained soil which is fertile is crucial.

Position: Plant the bulbs in sun in borders or by the terrace.

Care: Plant in late summer. Bulbs may rot in wet conditions. Ensure good drainage and plant tilted to the side if doubtful.

157

Galanthus nivalis '**Flore Pleno**': Snowdrop

This is the double-flowered form which grows vigorously into clumps, though it is not as spreading as the single-flowered form, as it is sterile. The snowdrop flowers are borne in late winter and the grey-green leaves die down in spring. Of the single-flowered snowdrops, 'Magnet' and 'S. Arnott' are both vigorous and have large flowers.

Height × spread: 10 × 10cm/4 × 4in

Soil: It enjoys moist soil that is well-drained with some humus.

Position: Plant in half-shade in the border. It will also naturalize in a wild corner.

Care: Plants can be divided and re-planted when in leaf.

◐ ◖ ❋❋❋

Gazania hybrids

These half-hardy annuals provide a succession of brilliantly coloured daisies, often zoned in a contrasting colour, from summer to autumn. Different forms are available, including the Mini-Star Series which is neat and compact, with orange, yellow, bronze, pink, white and beige rayed flowers, and glossy green leaves, silky white beneath. They are well-suited to containers.

Height × spread: 20 × 20cm/8 × 8in

Soil: Best in light, well-drained soil. They hate winter wet.

Position: A bright addition to containers in full sun or bedded out at the front of a border. They close up in dull weather.

Care: Plant out after frost is over. Deadhead regularly to encourage flowering.

Gentiana acaulis: Trumpet gentian

A prostrate, evergreen perennial with rich, dark-blue, trumpet flowers in late spring and early summer. There is also a white-flowered form. The leaves are deep green and glossy, forming a mat from which the short-stemmed flowers look up, exposing throats which are often speckled with green. It is worth re-planting elsewhere if not flowering well.

Height × spread: 7.5 × 30cm/3in × 1ft

Soil: It needs moist but well-drained soil, well supplied with humus.

Position: Grow in a rock garden or in a raised bed, or in a trough.

Care: In hot, dry summers it may need shade from the sun.

○ ◐ E ❋❋❋

Geranium cinereum 'Ballerina'

One of the prettiest hardy geraniums which makes a lovely front-of-border subject, especially spilling on to paving. This perennial produces red-veined mauve, dark-eyed flowers in late spring to early summer. The leaves form a low cushion, of soft greyish-green and deeply lobed. It is a good rock garden plant and floriferous.

Height × spread: 15 × 30cm/6in × 1ft

Soil: Easy in well-drained but moist soil, fairly fertile.

Position: It can be grown in a container or in a border, so long as it is in sun.

Care: Cut off spent flowering stems; and dead leaves to base.

◯ ◊ ❄❄❄

Geranium clarkei 'Kashmir Purple'

This is a hardy geranium with an indefinite spread so is not for tiny gardens. When it is kept under control in less restricted areas, it makes a very good edging plant providing speedy ground cover. In early to late summer it bears glowing, red-veined, purple flowers, white at the centre, over finely divided mid-green leaves.

Height × **spread:** 45 × 60+cm/1¹/₂ × 2+ft

Soil: Tolerant of most soils, though preferably fertile and well drained.

Position: For the front of beds, or in wilder corners.

Care: Deadhead. Watch for excessive spreading and dig out rhizomes if necessary.

○ ◑ | ◊ | ✱✱✱

Geranium psilostemon

Flowers of brilliant magenta with dark eyes from early to late summer and decorative foliage, colouring in autumn, make this a showy hardy perennial beside a patio. The leaves which are of mid-green have five lobes. It is a tough plant which will naturalize even in grass, and the flowers should be cut off before seeding if this is undesirable.

Height × spread: 1m × 60cm/3 × 2ft

Soil: Easy in well-drained, fairly fertile soils.

Position: In full sun it will gently self-seed in gravel, making in time a decorative colony. A good border plant.

Care: Deadhead. Cut down at the end of the year.

◯ ◊ ❄❄❄

Gladiolus callianthus

A half-hardy bulb with strap-like leaves and scented white
flowers with maroon markings in late summer and early
autumn. These flowers are held in loose, slightly drooping
sprays, several per stem, each attached with a short tube.
It is this that makes a group of these bulbs so graceful. Try
a generous number in a large pot.

Height × spread: 75 × 5cm/2¹/₂ft × 2in

Soil: Light, well-drained soil is suitable.

Position: For a large container or in a hot, sheltered position near the
house in the ground.

Care: Plant bulbs in spring after frosts. Liquid fertilize in growth. Lift
and over-winter in warmth.

Gladiolus × *colvillei* 'The Bride'

A frost-hardy bulb with flowers of white, pink or peach, often dark-feathered, in early summer, and rushy green leaves. This white form is called 'The Bride'. Other hybrids include 'Amanda Mahy' with salmon-pink flowers, 'Nymph' which is white with crimson markings and 'Spitfire' which is a striking red with flecks. They are good cut flowers.

Height × spread: 45 × 5cm/1½ft × 2in

Soil: Light, well-drained soil is suitable.

Position: They need full sun and take up little space in beds amongst perennials.

Care: Plant deeply in autumn and protect for winter.

| ◐ | ◊ | ✳✳ |

Gypsophila 'Rosy Veil'

A mid- to late summer-blooming plant with tiny blush double flowers forming a cloudy effect en masse and thin, grey-green leaves. Here it is shown with the seed heads of *Allium cristophii* (p. 110). It is a good plant for a rock garden, or in gravel, so long as it is given an open and sunny spot.

Height × spread: 45 × 75cm/1 1/2 × 2 1/2 ft

Soil: For light, well-drained alkaline soil, though it tolerates some moisture.

Position: Pretty beside paving in full sun, or at the front of a bed.

Care: To prevent straggliness, cut back the wiry stems in spring.

| ◯ | ◊ | Semi-E | ❋❋❋ |

Hedychium gardnerianum: Ginger lily

A tender perennial with large, green, spear-shaped leaves sprouting in spring from its rhizomes, and poker heads of scented creamy flowers in late summer to autumn. Bright red stamens protrude prominently from the flowers. In a sheltered position the rhizomes will spread freely, often near the surface and these must be fully protected in winter. It may survive.

Height × spread: 1.2 × 1m/4 × 3ft

Soil: For humus-rich soil that is moist but well-drained.

Position: Shelter by a hot wall where it can be thickly mulched in winter. A good plant by a patio.

Care: Protect in winter. Ensure it does not lack moisture in summer.

◖ ◗ ❄

Helleborus argutifolius: Corsican hellebore

A wonderful vigorous, evergreen perennial with
architectural dark green leaves and heads of clustered,
large, pale green flowers in later winter and spring with
golden stamens. The quality of leaves – leathery and spiny
along the edges – makes this one of the most worthwhile
year-round foliage plants in the garden. Once planted,
allow it to develop undisturbed.

Height × spread: 60 × 60cm/2 × 2ft

Soil: Easy in almost any neutral to alkaline soil.

Position: Plant by a terrace or with small shrubs, or at the front of a border.

Care: Add leaf-mould or compost when planting and in autumn each year. Deadhead.

| ○ | ◌ | E | ❋❋❋ |

Helleborus foetidus: Stinking hellebore

This perennial only smells when its dark green, finely cut leaves are crushed. It is very useful as an underplanting to a deciduous tree or in shady corners on patios where it will self-sow. Its ice-green flower bells with maroon rims last from late winter to late spring. It tolerates considerable neglect, though a mulch with compost is worthwhile.

Height × spread: 45 × 45cm/1¹/₂ × 1¹/₂ft

Soil: Easy in neutral to alkaline soil.

Position: Best in part shade or full shade. It may seed too enthusiastically on a gravel patio.

Care: Remove spent flowers or it will self-sow. Seedlings root deeply.

◑ ● | ◊ | E | ❄❄❄

Helleborus orientalis: Lenten rose

A top late-winter to spring-flowering perennial with handsome, dark green, deeply cut, tough leaves, which overwinter before dying, and saucer-shaped, single flowers with golden stamens, of variable colours, often spotted, including white, deep red, pink, yellow-green and near black. It has been much hybridized in recent years and double-flowered forms are now available.

Height × spread: 45 × 45cm/1¹/₂ × 1¹/₂ft

Soil: Heavy soil, neutral or with some lime, but they tolerate most soils unless very dry or waterlogged.

Position: Plant in part shade in a border or under deciduous trees.

Care: Add humus when planting and mulch every autumn. Cut off dead leaves.

◐ ◊ E ❄❄❄

Like other hybrid day lilies the light green, rushy leaves appear early in the year and are valuable in furnishing a border at a bleak time. Short-lived, soft-pink, trumpet flowers with green throats in summer are produced in continuous succession over a long period. Other forms are the dusky carmine 'Summer Wine' and the short, golden 'Stella de Oro'.

Height × spread: 75 × 75cm/2¹/₂ × 2¹/₂ft

Soil: Best in fertile, moist but well-drained soil.

Position: Plant as an edging by the patio or at the front of a border.

Care: Divide congested clumps. Deadhead, and cut down at end of year.

Hemerocallis lilioasphodelus: Day lily

A perennial with rushy leaves and such fragrant, golden, open-trumpet flowers in late spring to early summer that a clump by the patio will scent a whole area. It is rather later into leaf than most of the garden hybrids of day lilies, the foliage being dark green. Its fragrance is especially penetrating in the evening.

Height × spread: 75 × 75cm/2¹/₂ × 2¹/₂ft

Soil: Plant in moist well-drained soil, that is reasonably fertile.

Position: Place in a bed beside the patio, or at the front of a border.

Care: Divide congested clumps. Deadhead, and cut down at end of year.

◐ ◑ ❄❄❄

Hermodactylus tuberosus: Widow iris

A bulb with rushy, narrow, glaucous leaves and greenish-yellow flowers with dark velvety markings produced in spring. It has a strange, exotic appearance, and its other popular name is the snake's head iris. It can take a full year before establishing itself satisfactorily. The leaves will die back in early autumn and if needed the plant can be divided then.

Height × spread: 30 × 5cm/1ft × 2in

Soil: A well-drained soil which is limy.

Position: At the foot of a hot wall where it can be kept dryish in summer.

Care: Plant the tubers in autumn and guard against too much summer rain.

◐ ◊ ❄❄❄

Heuchera micrantha var. *diversifolia* 'Palace Purple'

A handsome dark-leafed evergreen with wands of tiny cream flowers in early summer. Another form with silver and purple leaves is called 'Persian Carpet'. The foliage of both plants is similarly lobed, forming the effect of a pointed, scalloped edge. Both are valuable in purple colour schemes or as a foil to silver leafed plants.

Height × **spread:** 45 × 45cm/1$\frac{1}{2}$ × 1$\frac{1}{2}$ft

Soil: It enjoys moist fertile soils.

Position: Use as a front-of-border or container plant but don't let it dry out in sun.

Care: Deadhead. Mulch in autumn every year. Remove dead leaves.

◗ ◑ ● | ◊ | E | ❄❄❄

Hosta 'Gold Standard': Plantain lily

Many of the gold-leafed hostas fade in colour but this cultivar retains its colour well. This perennial forms a clump of green-gold leaves edged with a dark green. Spikes of funnel-shaped lavender flowers rise in summer. In good earth, enriched with compost, it will form fine clumps. It can be divided in spring, but dislikes disturbance.

Height × spread: 60 × 60cm/2 × 2ft

Soil: It needs moist soil which is fertile and enriched with humus.

Position: For the edges of beds and among shrubs. Also use in containers.

Care: Mulch in spring. Guard against slugs which will ruin foliage. Deadhead. Remove dead leaves.

The much loved, very fragrant bulb with bell-flowers of blue, pink, crimson, purple, orange, yellow or white in early spring. A number of distinctive forms have become available in recent years including the beetroot-coloured 'Distinction', less stubby than the usual hyacinth and the lovely salmon-orange 'Gipsy Queen'. Both are good planted in groups.

Height × spread: 30 × 8cm/1ft × 3in

Soil: Any reasonably well-drained fertile soil.

Position: Container or bedding subjects but place in sun and where the bulbs won't suffer from excessive winter rain.

Care: Plant in early autumn. Protect container-grown bulbs from heavy winter rain.

Iberis umbellata: Common candytuft

A little hardy annual, foolproof to grow from seed, with
scented white, lilac, pink, purple or red flowers from
summer to early autumn. There are various strains that are
available from seedsmen including 'Fairy' which is a
miniature form, very compact, and 'Flash', slightly taller,
both in the full colour range. They make good edging
plants.

Height × spread: 15 × 30cm/6in × 1ft

Soil: It will grow almost anywhere in neutral to alkaline soil.

Position: Scatter the seed amongst paving or at the front of borders to
fill up gaps.

Care: Sow the seed in spring or autumn in situ.

○ ◊ ❄❄❄

177

Impatiens **hybrids**: Busy Lizzie

Tender perennials which are usually grown as annuals, with double or single flowers in a wide range of colours from early summer to autumn. They are all-purpose plants and tolerant of shady conditions. There are various strains including the Cleopatra Series which are early, compact and uniform. 'Mega Orange Star' tolerates extremes of weather.

Height × spread: 30 × 15cm/1ft × 6in

Soil: Moist but well-drained soil with some humus.

Position: Plant in hanging baskets, or other containers, or use as bedding, in a sheltered position.

Care: Plant out after frost. Shelter from wind.

◐ ◑ E ❄

Ipheion 'Rolf Fiedler'

A bulb with clumps of narrow, rushy leaves and scented, starry, blue flowers in spring. It is best grown in a container. It is not reliably hardy. *Ipheion uniflorum* is not fully hardy either but if protected in winter should make large clumps at the front of a bed. It has starry, silver-blue flowers, and there is a white form, *I. uniflorum* 'Album'.

Height × spread: 15 × 7.5cm/6 × 3in

Soil: Grow in well-drained soil with some humus.

Position: Lovely in a container in a sunny, sheltered site, protected from frost.

Care: Plant in autumn. Mulch for protection or winter indoors.

◯ ◌ ❄❄

Ipomoea lobata: Spanish flag

A tender perennial climber, grown as a half-hardy annual with tubular red flowers, later orange-yellow, from summer to autumn. This gives a decorative two-tone appearance to the flower spike. The leaves are lobed, pale or mid-green. It is a vigorous plant in good soil and will give a temporary clothing to a pergola.

Height × spread: 2–5m/6–15ft

Soil: Fairly fertile, well-drained soil, watered in the growing season.

Position: Plant out to grow on a support by a sunny wall after frosts are over.

Care: Sow in spring, chipping seed to aid germination. Plant out after frost.

Iris danfordiae

A little bulb with large, bright yellow flowers in late winter or early spring which makes a welcome show at this time. The leaves are thin, green and pointed. It usually flowers well after the first planting then the bulbs, which tend to break up, need lifting and growing on separately to flowering size.

Height × spread: 15 × 5cm/6 × 2in

Soil: Plant in well-drained soil.

Position: Lovely in containers which should be placed in full sun.

Care: Plant the bulbs in early autumn. Allow leaves to die down.

◑ ◊ ❋❋❋

Iris, Dutch

These are hybrid iris bulbs which are vigorous and glamorous with linear leaves and blue, violet, or yellow flowers in late spring or early summer. (The Dutch, English and Spanish irises are all related as they are hybrids of *I. xiphium*.) They are usually fairly cheap to buy and Dutch irises make good cut flowers. 'Purple Sensation' and 'Golden Harvest' are good forms.

Height × spread: 60 × 10cm/2ft × 4in

Soil: Easy in well-drained soil.

Position: Plant in groups around the patio or in beds in full sun.

Care: Plant in autumn; deadhead; and mulch for winter protection in very cold regions.

| ◯ | ◌ | ✳✳✳ |

Iris 'J. S. Dijt'

A choice small bulb belonging to the *Iris reticulata* group with flowers of richest red-purple with orange markings in early spring. There are a number of other good cultivars among this group including 'Harmony', sky-blue with orange markings, flowering before its leaves appear; 'Pauline' which is reddish-violet with white markings; and 'Clairette', pale-blue, violet and white.

Height × spread: 12 × 5cm/5 × 2in

Soil: For reasonably fertile well-drained soil.

Position: Plant in a bowl or in a trough for alpines or at the front of beds.

Care: Plant the bulbs in autumn. Allow leaves to die off naturally.

Iris 'Joyce'

A small bulb with blue flowers with yellow throats in early spring. It belongs to the *I. reticulata* group, blooming at a time when few other bulbs are in full display. The leaves are linear and mid-green, extending fully after the flowers have gone over. The bulbs tend to perform well the first season after planting, then split up.

Height × spread: 12 × 5cm/5 × 2in

Soil: For reasonably fertile well-drained soil, preferably alkaline.

Position: Plant in a bowl, or a trough for alpine plants or at the front of beds.

Care: Plant the bulbs in autumn. Allow leaves to die off naturally.

○ ◊ ❄❄❄

Lampranthus spectabilis

A tender showy succulent with fleshy, grey-green, slightly
curving leaves and magenta daisy flowers in summer and
early autumn. They are spectacular because of their
quantity and the fact that they are almost luminous. In
frost-free areas they can be planted out and will spread.
Otherwise they can be used only in containers and
wintered in frost-free conditions.

Height × spread: 30 × 45cm/1 × 1½ft

Soil: Needs very well-drained, light, poor soil.

Position: In frost-prone areas plant in containers for summer. Bring in
before frost.

Care: Deadhead regularly. Winter in frost-free conditions.

◖ ◊ E ❄

Lathyrus grandiflorus

A beautiful herbaceous climber with purple and pink flowers in summer in abundance. It is fully hardy. It has mid-green leaves and a spreading, suckering habit. Its season of flowering is shorter than that of its relative, *L. latifolius*, but the colour of its two-tone flowers is richer and they are produced in great quantity. They can be used for cutting.

Height: Climbing to 1.5m/5ft

Soil: For fertile, well-drained soil that does not dry out.

Position: A splendid showy plant against a wall in sun.

Care: Deadhead spent flowers. Cut dead stems to base in autumn, and dig out excessive spread.

○ ◐ ❄❄❄

Lathyrus latifolius: Everlasting pea

A slightly ramshackle in habit but beautiful herbaceous climber with glaucous leaves and magenta (or pure white) flowers from summer to early autumn. The foliage is blue-green and the plant climbs by leaf tendrils. It is a typical old cottage plant and even in a city garden, it will give a relaxed effect on walls or scrambling through shrubs.

Height: Climbing to 2m/6ft

Soil: For fairly fertile, well-drained soil that does not dry out.

Position: A good plant for tying against a wall in sun or part shade.

Care: Cut off dead flowers. Cut dead stems to the base in late autumn.

Laurentia axillaris: Rock isotome

A pretty little bushy but delicate plant grown as a half-hardy annual with finely cut pale green leaves and blue flowers all summer. There is also a white variety. The flowers are like butterflies and are produced in profusion, individually small, on top of a long pale tube. They are lightly scented in early evening or after a shower.

Height × **spread:** 15 × 30cm/6in × 1ft

Soil: Reasonably fertile, moist but well-drained light soil.

Position: Use for edging, or for a container or hanging basket in full sun.

Care: Sow at the beginning of the year and plant out after frost.

Lavatera trimestris 'Silver Cup': Mallow

One of the most showy mallows, a hardy annual with silver-green leaves and veined, rose-coloured flowers all summer on a bushy plant with a substantial presence. Other cultivars are white, called 'Mont Blanc', or the blush, dark-centred 'Pink Beauty' or 'Ruby Regis' which has 10cm/4in flowers of rich cerise.

Height × spread: 75 × 45cm/2¹/₂ × 1¹/₂ft

Soil: For well-drained soil which is light and fairly fertile.

Position: Plant in full sun in containers or in open ground. It is usually grown from seed in spring.

Care: Sow the seed in situ in mid- or late spring.

Lewisia cotyledon hybrids

These are dwarf, hardy, evergreen perennials with fleshy leaves and flowers of pink, purple, orange, yellow and white, slightly funnel-shaped, held in sprays on stems rising above the basal rosette of foliage. They are hardy but the crown is liable to rot in excessive winter wet. They are best grown on a slope or protected from heavy winter rain.

Height × spread: Up to 30 × 25cm/1ft × 10in

Soil: It needs very well-drained neutral or acid soil; in a container, part loam, leaf mould and grit or sharp sand.

Position: Grow in full sun or in very light shade in a rock crevice, on a slope or in a trough.

Care: Protect from winter wet which is liable to cause neck rot.

○ ◐ | ◌ | E | LH | ❊❊❊

Lilium African Queen Group: Lily

Trumpet lilies with yellow, apricot or orange interiors, darker on the reverse, whose pyramids of midsummer flowers will scent the patio. It is not reliably hardy but, like many other hybrid lilies, is excellent in containers. The flowers are excellent for cutting. In any case, spent flower heads should be cut off but the stems allowed to die down naturally.

Height: 1.2–2m/4–6ft

Soil: For moist but well-drained soil, humus-rich, which is well fed.

Position: Plant deeply in a container or a border in a sheltered position.

Care: Plant and protect in late autumn. Liquid fertilize regularly and water well when in growth. Deadhead.

191

Lilium 'Golden Splendor': Lily

Most lilies are very good in containers where the bulbs are protected from mice etc. This is a Trumpet type with rich gold scented flowers in midsummer, which are suffused with burgundy-red on the reverse of the petals. It is vigorous and sturdy but may need staking or tying to a support. All tall lilies need shelter.

Height: 1.2m/4ft

Soil: For fertile humus-rich but well-drained soil that is well fed.

Position: Plant deeply in a container or in a border in shelter.

Care: Plant in late autumn. Liquid fertilize and water well when in growth. Deadhead.

○ ◑ │ ◇ │ ❋❋❋

Lilium 'King Pete': Lily

A very robust Asiatic hybrid bulb with open flowers of gold shading to orange, with spots nearer the centre, in summer. It will spread vigorously though is often happier in a container than in open ground. Like all lilies, good drainage is paramount for its success though it also needs soil that does not dry out. It is floriferous.

Height: 1m/3ft

Soil: For fertile, moist but well-drained soil.

Position: Plant deeply in containers or open ground.

Care: Plant in late autumn to winter. Liquid fertilize and water in growth. Deadhead.

◐ ◊ ❋❋❋

Lilium longiflorum: Easter lily

A favourite tender florist's lily with very large, fragrant, white, trumpet flowers produced in midsummer and spears of dark green leaves. It is an excellent flower for cutting but makes one of the most dramatic-looking lilies for containers as the trumpets can grow to nearly 20cm/8in long. The pot must be kept in frost-free conditions.

Height: 45–60cm/1½–2ft

Soil: Moist and rich but well-drained soil. This lily will tolerate some lime.

Position: Plant deeply in a container for which it is well suited.

Care: It must be given frost-free conditions. Liquid fertilize and water well when in growth. Deadhead.

194

Lilium 'Mont Blanc': Lily

A reliable Asiatic hybrid with upward-turned, open flowers of cream, lightly spotted with brown, in early to midsummer. It will form a clump whether in a pot or in the open ground and is vigorous. It is an easy lily and its size makes it especially suitable for being grown in containers. Its colour is also a good mixer.

Height: 60–75cm/2–2¹/₂ft

Soil: For fertile, moist but well-drained soil.

Position: Plant deeply in a container or in a border.

Care: Plant in late autumn. Liquid fertilize and water well when in growth. Deadhead.

Lilium 'Olivia': Lily

One of the loveliest bulbs with large, fragrant, snow-white, bowl-shaped flowers in midsummer or later and dark green leaves. It is an Oriental hybrid. A group in a large bowl makes a magnificent display and will not need staking. As with all lilies, drainage is essential and in a pot a layer of grit at the base is helpful.

Height: 75cm–1m/2–3ft

Soil: For fertile, humus-rich, well-drained but moist soil that is neutral to acid and well fed.

Position: Plant deeply in a container or in a border.

Care: Plant in late autumn. Liquid fertilize and water well when in growth. Deadhead.

◐◑ ◊ ⃞LH⃞ ❋❋❋

Lilium 'Pink Perfection': Lily

A reliable Trumpet hybrid lily with large, very scented flowers of rich purple-pink in midsummer, borne on tall, strong stems which are liable to need some form of support. Staking is better if it is as unobtrusive as possible. In any case, these lilies should never be used in a position where they are subject to wind.

Height: 1.2–1.5m/4–5ft

Soil: For fertile, humus-rich, well-drained but moist soil which is well fed.

Position: Plant deeply in a container or in the border.

Care: Plant in late autumn. Liquid fertilize and water well when in growth. Deadhead.

Lilium regale: Regal lily

A beautiful and reliable perennial bulb which has very fragrant white trumpet flowers, purplish on the outside, produced in midsummer. It is good in part-shady positions as well as sun and excellent in the border, though well adapted to being grown in a pot where like all lilies it looks better in a group of at least three.

Height: 60cm–2m/2–6ft

Soil: For moist but well-drained soil, humus-rich, which is well fed:

Position: Plant deeply in a container or in a border.

Care: Plant in late autumn. Liquid fertilize and water well when in growth. Deadhead.

◐◑ △ ✳✳✳

Lilium speciosum var. rubrum: Lily

A very valuable reliable species of lily for its late summer to early autumn scented blooms, ten or more to each stem, with reflexed turkscap petals of carmine and white, spotted with deep rose. The flower opens flat initially before each petal recurves. Prominent stamens, entirely exposed, are a feature. It is fairly vigorous and will clump up well.

Height: 1.2m/4ft

Soil: This lily is best in humus-rich moist soil that is acidic.

Position: Plant deeply in part shade, in a container or a border.

Care: Plant in late autumn to late winter. Liquid fertilize and water well in growth. Deadhead.

◐ ◊ LH ❋❋❋

A larger-flowered version of *L. speciosum* var. *rubrum* with more imposing deep pink and white, scented blooms in late summer. It is well placed near silver foliage plants. The blooms are heavily spotted with crimson, and produced in profusion. Like most lilies, it dislikes disturbance. It may need some form of support and it is ideal if this can be unobtrusive.

Height: 1–1.5m/3–5ft

Soil: For humus-rich moist soil that is acidic.

Position: Plant deeply in a container or in a border in part shade.

Care: Plant in late autumn. Liquid fertilize and water well when in growth. Deadhead.

◑ ◐ LH ❄❄❄

Lilium 'Stargazer': Lily

An Oriental hybrid lily which is one of the most exotic and eye-catching in its group with rich carmine spotted flowers of an open, starry formation, with a thin white margin and prominently displayed stamens. It has a heady fragrance and is particularly suited to being grown in a container in a group of at least three.

Height: 1–1.5m/3–5ft

Soil: For rich, moist but well-drained soil which is neutral to acid.

Position: Plant deeply in a container or in a border.

Care: Plant in late autumn. Liquid fertilize and water well when in growth. Deadhead.

○ ◑ | ◊ | LH | ❄❄❄

Linaria maroccana **'Fairy Lights'**: Toadflax

A sprightly little hardy annual with a profusion of purple, yellow and white lipped flowers in summer covering the narrow-leafed bush. Other hues of this tiny flower are pink, orange or carmine, with contrasting white throats. 'Northern Lights' is a strain in the same colour range, but is long-flowering, twice as tall and excellent as a group. They are easy from seed.

Height × **spread:** 30 × 15cm/1ft × 6in

Soil: Easy in light, especially sandy soil, which is fairly fertile.

Position: For gravel, and beds and gaps among paving where it can be sown and will also self-seed.

Care: Sow the seed in spring in situ.

○ ◊ ❀❀❀

Lobelia erinus

There are many cultivars of these compact or trailing
tender perennials with green or bronze leaves and small,
blue, carmine, violet, pink or white flowers all summer to
autumn. The bushy forms are normally used for edging
and they include the strain 'Mrs Clibran' which is deep
blue with a white edge. Trailing forms are normally used
for hanging baskets.

Height × spread: 15 × 20cm/6 × 8in or more

Soil: It needs moist, well-fertilized soil to flower well.

Position: Plant as an edging or to trail from boxes or hanging
baskets.

Care: Plant out after frost. Feed with a liquid fertilizer.

Lotus berthelotii: Parrot's beak

Grown usually as a beautiful tender, trailing annual
(though perennial), with glistening silver, hairy, needle
leaves and brilliant red claw-like flowers in spring and
early summer or later. These flowers are presented either
in pairs or singly. In frost-free areas it can be used for
ground cover. Elsewhere it is almost always grown in a
container. It can be trimmed for bushiness.

Height × spread: 20cm × 1m/8in × 3ft

Soil: Best in light, gritty and well-drained fairly fertile soil.

Position: Plant in full sun in hanging baskets or containers to trail over
the sides.

Care: Plant outside only after frosts are past. Trim for neatness if
wanted.

Lychnis yunnanensis

A very easy semi-evergreen, grassy-leafed perennial which produces a show of brilliant rose-coloured flowers in clusters on stems in late spring to summer. It comes from Yunnan, West China and has only been introduced in recent years for widely available cultivation, yet is one of the best and neatest of the *Lychnis* species.

Height × spread: 30–45 × 30–45cm/1–1 1/2 × 1–1 1/2ft

Soil: Easy in almost any well-drained soil that is fairly fertile.

Position: Plant at the front of borders, in gravel or amongst paving.

Care: Cut off the spent flowerheads, stems and dead leaves.

◯ ◌ Semi-E ❄❄❄

Matthiola incana: Stocks

Very scented plants, much hybridized, grown as annuals
or biennials with single or double flowers in crimson,
pink, mauve, purple, white, salmon or soft yellow,
clustering in spikes above soft, greyish-green leaves. The
biennials flower in spring onwards, those grown as
annuals or half-hardy annuals in summer onwards. The
low-growing Cinderella Series is fully double and clove-
sweet.

Height × spread: 20–45 × 20cm/8in–1 ¹/₂ft × 8in

Soil: It needs moist, well-drained and fertile soil, neutral or with some
lime.

Position: Plant out in sun and shelter as bedding or use in containers.

Care: Sow the biennials in summer, plant out in spring. Sow annuals
early under glass or outside in spring.

◯ ◌ ✳✳/✳✳✳

Mentha × *gracilis* 'Variegata': Ginger mint

A vigorous spreading mint with decorative, aromatic, green-and-gold-striped or marked leaves and whorls of tiny lilac flowers in summer. The leaves are occasionally used to decorative effect in salads. Its roots may run excessively in the ground, so rather than grow it in a herb garden it can be used as a foliage plant for a pot.

Height × spread: 30cm × 1m/1 × 3ft

Soil: Give this mint moist, poor soil.

Position: Grow in part or full shade and contain its vigour in a pot.

Care: Cut the old stems to the base in late autumn.

Mentha suaveolens 'Variegata': Pineapple mint

A vigorous spreading mint which is decorative if well-contained in a pot. Aromatic, soft green leaves are splashed and sometimes entirely cream-coloured. Insignificant cream flower spikes appear in summer. By this time the plant will be beginning to sprawl and it will keep better shape if these flowering shoots are kept pinched out.

Height × spread: 1 × 1m/3 × 3ft

Soil: It is well adapted to cope with poor, moist soil.

Position: Grow in part or full shade in a container.

Care: Cut the old stems to the base in late autumn.

◐ ● | 🌢 | ❊❊❊

Miscanthus sinensis 'Silver Feather'

A big grass can make a big effect in a small space, sited here behind a seat. It makes an ornamental perennial clump sending up stems of green leaves in late spring, arching beneath plumes of silver panicles of flowers on strong stems which are produced in autumn, lasting the winter. *M.s.* 'Zebrinus' is shorter and has horizontal yellow bands across its leaves.

Height × spread: 2.5 × 2.5cm/8 × 6ft

Soil: Very easy in most fairly fertile soils, moist but well-drained.

Position: Plant in sun, ideally as a specimen.

Care: Cut down the dead stems in spring and, if spreading too much, dig out excess growth.

| ○ | ◐ | ❄❄❄ |

Muscari aucheri: Oxford and Cambridge grape hyacinth

A choice variety of grape hyacinth in which the spikes of spring flowers are brighter blue at the top, darkening at the base, their stems emerging from grassy leaves. The bulbs spread but are unlikely to self-sow. It is not invasive like the ordinary form of bright blue grape hyacinth, *M. armeniacum*, which is liable to take over parts of a small garden.

Height × spread: 15 × 5cm/6 × 2in

Soil: Easy in well-drained but moist soil which is fairly fertile.

Position: Plant amongst other spring-flowering bulbs in the ground, rock garden or in containers.

Care: If the bulbs become congested. lift and re-plant them in summer.

◯ ◑ | ◊ | ✷✷✷

Narcissus 'Hawera': Daffodil

An enchanting small daffodil, not completely hardy, with pendant soft yellow flower-heads with reflexed petals, several per stem, and slim foliage clumps. It belongs to the Triandrus division. So does the taller milk-white *Narcissus* 'Thalia' with several flowers per stem. This will clump up well in a bed. It is fully hardy and will give a fine prolonged display.

Height × spread: 18 × 7.5cm/7 × 3in

Soil: For well-drained soil, moist in spring and fairly fertile.

Position: Plant in containers which can be sheltered in winter, or in a protected spot outside.

Care: Plant in autumn. Cut off spent flowers but not the leaves until six weeks after flowering.

◐ ◊ ✳✳

The trumpet of this double daffodil is frilled, close-packed with pink and apricot segments, surrounded by white petals (perianth segments). It has grey-green leaves. Other beautiful double-flowered forms are the white and buttercream 'Irene Copeland' and 'Flower Drift' which has white petals and egg-yellow and orange central segments and will naturalize well in grass.

Height × spread: 45 × 10cm/1 ¹/₂ft × 4in

Soil: For well-drained soil, moist in the spring, and fairly fertile.

Position: Plant in containers or in beds where the trumpet cup can be seen.

Care: Plant in autumn. Deadhead spent flowers. Don't cut the leaves down for at least six weeks after flowering.

◐ ◇ ❋❋❋

Narcissus 'Roseworthy': Daffodil

A vigorous large-cupped narcissus with a salmon-pink trumpet and white petals and grey-green foliage. It will make good clumps in a short time. Like other daffodils with a pink trumpet it needs placing with care as its apricot-pink colour clashes slightly with spring flowers of lavender-pink. It will naturalize in grass.

Height × spread: 30 × 7.5cm/1ft × 3in

Soil: For fairly fertile drained soil, moist in spring.

Position: Plant in spaces amongst herbaceous plants or shrubs.

Care: Plant in autumn. Cut off spent flowers but not the leaves until six weeks after flowering.

◐ ◑ | ◊ | ✽✽✽

Nemesia caerulea

A half-hardy perennial with variably coloured small-lipped flowers of blue, pink, mauve or white from early summer to autumn and small green leaves. It will self-sow lightly where happy. It is a quieter more refined plant than the brightly coloured, bushy, small half-hardy annual *N. strumosa*, which is used for bedding and containers.

Height × spread: Up to 45 × 30cm/1¹/₂ × 1ft

Soil: It prefers light, well-drained slightly acid soil.

Position: Plant in containers, in raised beds or at the front of small borders.

Care: Pinch out the growing tips to prevent straggliness. Protect in winter.

○ ◌ LH ❋❋

Nerine bowdenii

A valuable autumn-flowering bulb with pale green strap-like leaves and heads of glistening silvery pink (or white) flowers. It will spread into a clump of bulbs quite vigorously. It is also suitable for cutting and lasts well in water. There are several outstanding forms, including the taller 'Mark Fenwick' with larger rich pink flowers. The white form is called *N.b.* f. *alba*.

Height × spread: 45 × 7.5cm/1^1/$_2$ft × 3in

Soil: Grow in well-drained soil.

Position: Plant in full sun in a protected position in beds.

Care: Plant the bulbs in spring with the nose near the surface. Deadhead. Protect in winter.

| ◖ | ◌ | ❋❋❋ |

Nicotiana langsdorffii

A half-hardy annual with pendant tubular flowers all summer, sometimes to autumn, of ice-green with an open mouth. They are presented in sprays on a branching plant with a rosette of long deep green leaves at its base. It is very different in appearance from the common tobacco plant (*N. alata* hybrids) with scented open-mouthed flowers, variably coloured.

Height × spread: 1–1.2m × 30cm/3–4 × 1ft

Soil: For moist but well-drained soil which is fertile.

Position: Plant out after frosts are past in a border, or in a container in sun or part shade.

Care: Sow the seed in early spring and plant out when frosts are past.

◐ ◑ 💧 ❄

Nigella damascena: Love-in-a-mist

A charming and easy annual, grown from seed in situ in autumn for spring/summer-flowering, or in spring for summer/autumn-flowering, with feathery foliage and white, rose, dark blue or pale blue flowers (as in the form 'Miss Jekyll') followed by handsome seed pods. These seed pods are often dried for use by flower arrangers. The flowers are good for cutting.

Height × spread: 45 × 15cm/1¹/₂ft × 6in

Soil: It tolerates any reasonably fertile soil that is well-drained.

Position: Sow to form groups in a sunny border where it may gently self-seed.

Care: Autumn-sown seedlings may need winter protection in cold areas.

| ◖ | ◌ | ✲✲✲ |

Oenothera speciosa **'Pink Petticoats'**: Evening primrose

One of the most floriferous perennials, quickly spreading, with rosettes of green leaves and masses of pink flowers, darker veined, with white and gold centres carried successively from early summer to early autumn. Unlike many varieties of evening primrose its flowers are fully open in the day. *O. fruticans* 'Fireworks', with yellow blooms opening from red buds, is also a daytime bloomer.

Height × spread: 30 × 45cm/1 × 1¹/₂ft

Soil: Grow in well-drained, preferably gritty, poor or only fairly fertile soil.

Position: Plant in full sun as an edging plant in a bed or border.

Care: Protect the plant from too much winter wet. Watch that its runners aren't too invasive.

○ ◊ ❋❋❋

Osteospermum jucundum: African daisy

An almost hardy, compact perennial with a proliferation of rich pink, golden-centred daisy flowers rising on stems from neat clumps of lance-shaped grey-green leaves. It flowers from late spring until autumn. The form that is called *O.j.* var. *compactum* is slightly more dwarf. Another frost-hardy African daisy worth growing is *O. ecklonis*, white with an indigo reverse and disc.

Height × spread: 20 × 30cm/8in × 1ft

Soil: It needs light and well-drained soil, which is fairly fertile.

Position: Plant in shelter beside paving, in gravel, in containers, in raised beds or at the front of borders.

Care: Deadhead; and protect the plant in winter.

◯ ◊ E ❉❉

Paeonia lactiflora 'Bowl of Beauty': Peony

Peonies take a lot of space for a short season of flowering, but are so sumptuous that they are worth it. This one has large pink bowls stuffed with creamy yellow petaloids in high summer. Its mid-green leaves are deeply cut and make a foliage contribution. Like most peonies these leaves colour in autumn. 'Globe of Light' is another glorious cultivar.

Height × spread: 1 × 1m/3 × 3ft

Soil: For fertile, moist but well-drained soil, enriched with humus.

Position: Plant in full sun in borders among herbaceous plants or shrubs.

Care: Remove dead leaves and spent flower stems. Mulch. Do not disturb the plant.

🌑 💧 ❄❄❄

Papaver rhoeas: Annual poppy

The annual poppies are almost foolproof to grow from seed and will give any airy lightness to a small garden. They can be single or double, pink, purple, orange, or scarlet, sometimes with a black heart, sometimes edged or marked with flakes. *P. somniferum*, the opium poppy, is another foolproof annual, its huge blooms followed by large, glaucous seed-pods, good for flower arranging.

Height × spread: 45cm–1m × 30cm/1½–3 × 1ft

Soil: They need very well-drained soil that is quite fertile.

Position: Give them a sunny spot beside paving or in gaps in a bed.

Care: Sow the seed of annual poppies in spring in situ.

Pelargonium 'Barbe Bleu': Ivy-leafed geranium

A glamorous, tender, trailing pelargonium with ivy-form foliage and clusters of double, ruby-black flowers. It is much sought after. As with all trailing pelargoniums, it needs to be tied up or supported if it is required to climb. Their stems are also slightly brittle and break easily at the joints so they should not be put in a windy position.

Height × spread: 60 × 20cm/2ft × 8in

Soil: Easy in any soil which has some lime content or is neutral.

Position: Grow in shelter in sun in a tall container putting it outside only when frosts are past.

Care: Reduce water in winter and prune as needed. In summer feed with a balanced fertilizer and deadhead.

◯ ◊ E ❋

Pelargonium 'Paton's Unique': Unique geranium

A robust, tender, evergreen shrubby perennial which can be stood out in summer with scented leaves and clusters of warm pink flowers with a white centre. It belongs to the so-called Unique group of pelargoniums. Many of this section were popular in Victorian times. They are vigorous plants, often with aromatic leaves, and make good cool greenhouse plants. Some grow to 1.2m/4ft.

Height × spread: 45 × 30cm/1½ × 1ft

Soil: Easy in any fertile soil which is neutral to alkaline.

Position: Grow in sun in a container, putting it outside only when frosts are past.

Care: Reduce water in winter, and prune as needed. In summer feed with a balanced fertilizer and deadhead.

◯ ◌ E ❋

Pelargonium, **zonal**: Geranium

These tender evergreen perennials are often used as
container or bedding plants. Bushy and shrubby, their
leaves are marbled, often with darker zones, and they
flower from summer to autumn. The single or double
blooms are white, salmon, red, pink or purple, often
veined or blotched. There are innumerable cultivars, one
of the prettiest being the dwarf 'Apple Blossom Rosebud'.

Height × spread: 60 × 45cm/2 × 1¹/₂ft

Soil: They prefer well-drained but moist soil, neutral or with some lime.

Position: Plant in sun in containers after frost is past, or use for beds.

Care: Deadhead regularly to promote flowering. Lift and overwinter
indoors.

Penstemon 'Stapleford Gem'

A long-flowering perennial with subtly coloured pink, blue, lilac and white tubular flowers on spikes from summer to autumn and mid-green leaves. Other good varieties are 'Apple Blossom' and 'Blackbird' which is a rich maroon. These are all reasonably hardy except in severe conditions. A hardier variety for gardeners in cold areas is 'Evelyn' with small pink tubular flowers and thin leaves.

Height × spread: 60 × 45cm/2 × 1½ft

Soil: It needs well-drained soil which is fertile.

Position: Plant in a bed or border in full sun.

Care: Deadhead to prolong the flowering and prune only in spring in cold areas.

◻ ◊ ❋❋❋

Petunia hybrids

Invaluable showy, saucer- or trumpet-flowered, half-hardy annuals blooming from late spring to late autumn in pink, ruby, purple, white or yellow, sometimes striped or veined. They are drought-resistant. The form photographed belongs to the Surfinia Series, a vigorous and branching strain of Grandiflora petunias, single or double, which produce long trailing stems. They are resistant to wet weather.

Height × spread: 30cm × 30cm–1m/1 × 1–3ft

Soil: They need good drainage and a light loamy soil.

Position: Plant in containers or hanging baskets, always in full sun in a protected position.

Care: Plant out after risk of frost. Water when in growth.

| ○ | ◊ | ❄ |

Phlox subulata: Moss phlox

An evergreen mat or mounded plant with thin, bright green leaves and flowers of red, pink, violet or mauve in late spring and early summer. The vigorous cultivar shown is 'McDaniel's Cushion' with large pink flowers. There are a number of other beautiful easy rock phlox including the similar *P. douglasii*, which can also be used to make evergreen mats.

Height × spread: 5 × 45cm/2in × 1 1/2ft

Soil: For fertile soil that is well-drained.

Position: Plant beside paving or in gravel, front-of-border or in a raised bed.

Care: Clip lightly after flowering.

| ◐ | ◊ | E | ❅❅❅ |

Phuopsis stylosa

A useful, very spreading, evergreen perennial which will form a ground-cover mat of pale green thin leaves surmounted by a succession of rounded pink flowerheads for a long time in summer. It is quick growing and if cut back after its prolonged first flush it may produce a second crop of flowers in autumn. It is useful planted in paving.

Height × spread: 15 × 60cm/6in × 2ft

Soil: Easy in gritty soil, well-drained, but moist.

Position: Plant at the edge of a raised bed, in gravel, on sloping ground or by paving.

Care: Clip after flowering to maintain neatness.

◯◑ △ E ❄❄❄

Pratia pedunculata

A useful prostrate creeper for paving crevices with tiny, pale blue flower stars for a long period in summer on short stalks above mats of small evergreen leaves. It will spread vigorously, rooting as it develops. It is a good plant to use among paving on a terrace. If it is started off here in a crevice, it won't be too invasive.

Height × spread: 2cm/1in × indefinite spread

Soil: It will grow in dry or in moist fairly fertile soil.

Position: Plant in paving gaps, or in rock gardens where you can tolerate a degree of invasion.

Care: If it spreads where unwanted, divide the plant at any season.

⊙ ◑ | ◌ | E | ❋❋❋

Primula auricula **hybrid**: Auricula

Auriculas are excellent subjects for the small garden as they are often grown in pots. These evergreen perennials have thick, pale green leaves, often white dusted, with numbers of yellow flowers (or variably mauve, purple or crimson, often margined in the hybrids) borne from spring to early summer. 'Red Dusty Miller' is an old favourite with red flowers and powdered leaves.

Height × spread: 20 × 25cm/8 × 10in

Soil: They thrive in moist, gritty, well-drained soil, with leaf mould.

Position: Plant in half-shade or in sun, if the soil is moist, in the border or in containers.

Care: Deadhead. It benefits from a mulch of humus in late winter.

◐ ◑ 🌢 E ❄❄❄

Primula Gold Laced Group

One of the jewels of the Primula-Polyanthus section, with darkest maroon, velvety flowers in spring, thinly margined with gold (or silver), and with gold centres, carried in umbels over mid-green clumps of leaves. It is apt to be short-lived and it will help if it is mulched. The plant can be divided between autumn and winter.

Height × spread: 25 × 30cm/10in × 1ft

Soil: Thrives best in neutral to acid soil, with leaf mould.

Position: Plant in part or dappled shade at the front of a bed.

Care: Deadhead. It can be short-lived and needs a rich mulch of humus in late winter.

❍◐ | 💧 | Semi-E | ❄❄❄

Primula 'Guinevere'

An indispensable, evergreen, perennial primrose, making spreading rosettes of bronze-green leaves, covered in spring with dainty, mauve-pink flowers with gold centres. It is a particularly easy hybrid and, if mulched, will form large clumps which are best divided every couple of years between autumn and spring. It is very floriferous and looks well beside pale blue pulmonarias.

Height × spread: 12 × 25cm/5 × 10in

Soil: It thrives best in neutral to acid soil, with leaf mould.

Position: Plant in part or dappled shade at the front of beds.

Care: It is easy but will benefit from a mulch of humus in late winter.

◑ ◐ E ❋❋❋

Primula vulgaris **'Miss Indigo'**: Double primrose

One of the most distinctive of the many cultivars of double primroses, with deep violet flowers, finely margined with white, carried in spring over rosettes of mid-green leaves. Other cultivars with double flowers are the lovely white 'Alba Plena' ('Double White') and the lilac 'Lilacina Plena'. *Primula* Hose in Hose has one single primrose flower emerging from the throat of another.

Height × spread: 20 × 20cm/8 × 8in

Soil: It thrives in neutral to acid soil, with leaf mould.

Position: Plant in part or dappled shade at the front of beds, or grow in a container.

Care: It benefits from a mulch of humus in late winter.

◑ ◐ | Semi-E | ❀❀❀

There are many forms of this perennial including 'Bowles' Blue', above, with icy blue bell-flowers in spring and clumps of evergreen white-spotted leaves. Other cultivars have white flowers. The ordinary variety which opens pink turning to blue, popularly called Soldiers and Sailors, spreads and self-sows too freely for the small garden, though forming good ground cover. The bluest lungwort is *P. angustifolia*.

Height × spread: 30 × 45cm/1 × 1¹/₂ft

Soil: Best in damp soil, not waterlogged, which has been enriched with humus.

Position: Plant at the front of shady beds, or near the house for early colour.

Care: Take off the old leaves after it has flowered. Divide clumps if needed every few years.

Pulsatilla vulgaris: Pasque flower

One of the loveliest spring-flowering perennials with finely divided green foliage and nodding or upright large bell flowers of purple, crimson, pale violet or white with golden stamens. Silky silver mophead seed-heads follow. The fern-like leaves tend to develop after flowering. Another choice species requiring similar conditions is *P. halleri* with large purple flowers with gold stamens, opening from woolly buds.

Height × spread: 20 × 20cm/8 × 8in

Soil: It needs fertile, light and very well-drained soil to succeed.

Position: Plant in full sun in a raised bed, in gravel or in a rock garden or by a well-drained patio.

Care: Plant when young as they resent being disturbed. Deadheading will improve continuity of flowering.

235

Puschkinia scilloides var. *libanotica*

A small bulb, flowering in late winter or early spring with milk blue flowers enhanced by a darker blue central stripe along each petal. The green basal leaves die down in late spring. There is a completely white form called 'Alba'. This bulb is a relative of both *Scilla* and *Chionodoxa*, whose spring-flowering species are also excellent in the small garden.

Height × spread: 15 × 5cm/6 × 2in

Soil: Easy in any well-drained soil.

Position: Plant in part shade or sun among shrubs or perennials, or can be grown in containers.

Care: If container-grown, to prevent mud splashing the pale flowers, spread a thin layer of grit over the pot.

◯ ◑ ◌ ❋❋❋

A lovely unusual perennial for cool places in a small garden with a succession of hooded, purple, or sometimes white, flowers in early and midsummer emerging from sheafs of rich green faintly ribbed leaves. Slugs love these leaves and precautions may need to be taken to prevent their being shredded. The bulbs are dormant from autumn to early summer.

Height × spread: 20 × 20cm/8 × 8in

Soil: It needs fertile, moist though well-drained peaty soil enriched with leaf-mould.

Position: Plant in shady, damp areas or in a small peat bed.

Care: In winter protect the tubers (which should be planted deeply) with a mulch.

◑ ◊ LH ❄❄/❄❄❄

Salvia farinacea 'Strata': Mealy sage

A newly popular and beautiful sage, usually grown as a half-hardy annual, with silver erect stems carrying small rich-blue flowers emerging from woolly, whitish calyces. Its leaves are a glossy mid-green, but are white-hairy on the undersides. It makes a bushy perennial in frost-free areas, flowering from summer to autumn. It originates from Mexico or Texas.

Height × spread: 45 × 30cm/1½ × 1ft

Soil: For well-drained, moist but fairly fertile soil.

Position: Plant in full sun as bedding, or use in containers.

Care: Sow seed in spring, planting out after risk of frost. Over-winter in frost-free conditions.

Salvia patens

A frost-tender perennial with soft, hairy, mid-green leaves and rich-blue lipped flowers on spikes in summer to autumn. It can be flowered in the same year if sown early as a half-hardy annual, or grown from tubers. There is a pale blue form too which is called 'Cambridge Blue'. Plant the tubers out after risk of frost is over.

Height × spread: 60 × 45cm/2 × 1¹/₂ft

Soil: For fairly fertile light, well-drained but moist soil with some humus.

Position: Plant in sun in containers, protected in winter, or in a sheltered site in the ground.

Care: Cut withered flowers/foliage down, lift the tubers or protect the plant in winter.

Saxifraga × *urbium*: London pride

A favourite cottage perennial with evergreen, toothed rosettes of leaves which spread vigorously into ground-covering mats and stems of starry pink and white flowers in early summer. In a tiny garden it will have to be under strict control because of its speed of growth, but few small evergreen plants are so easy in difficult spots and so neat in appearance.

Height × spread: 30cm/1ft × indefinite spread

Soil: One of the easiest plants, tolerating most conditions and soil, even poor.

Position: Plant as a front-of-border subject or beside paving.

Care: Cut off the spent flowering stems. Divide the plants if spreading where not required.

Schizanthus pinnatus hybrids: Butterfly flower

Showy half-hardy annuals with orchid-like flowers produced in abundance in yellow, pink, rose-red, purple or white, often with contrasting throats and marks from summer to autumn, on bushy dwarf plants. Its leaves are deeply divided and mid-green. Various forms have become popular, including 'Hit Parade' which is dense and bushy and 'Star Parade', dwarf and pyramidal.

Height × spread: 20–45 × 20–45cm/8in–1 1/2ft × 8in–1 1/2ft

Soil: Moist but well-drained soil is needed which is fairly fertile.

Position: After frosts are past, plant in full sun in containers or use as bedding plants.

Care: To increase bushiness, pinch back the young shoots.

Sedum 'Autumn Joy': Ice plant

A handsome fleshy perennial with pale grey-green leaves and stems with flat flower-heads that are ice-green in summer, turning rose to bronze-crimson by later summer to autumn. Neat in habit but can self-sow lightly. The spent flowering stems are usually cut down at the end of the year but, if left on, are decorative in winter.

Height × spread: 45 × 45cm/1 1/2 × 1 1/2ft

Soil: For well-drained soil, neutral or with some lime.

Position: Plant in full sun, by the patio or in gravel or at a border front.

Care: Cut off the dead flowering stems at the end of the year.

○ ◊ ❄❄❄

Sedum spathulifolium: Stonecrop

There are several forms of this creeping, hardy, evergreen which forms mats of fleshy leaves in rosettes of either greenish or silvery leaves, sometimes suffused with purple at the edges. Sprays of yellow flowers appear in summer. The form that is called 'Cape Blanco' is very silvery-grey due to the powder on its leaves. It is hardy, too.

Height × spread: 10 × 60cm/4in × 2ft

Soil: For well-drained soil, neutral or with some lime.

Position: Plant in full sun, in paving, beds or in containers.

Care: Cut off flowers and divide the plant if it is spreading too far.

| ○ | ◊ | E | ❄❄❄ |

Sempervivum tectorum: Houseleek

There are many cultivars of these evergreen succulent perennials with spreading rosettes of fleshy leaves. This form is called 'Limelight', a sharp acid green with pointed red-tipped leaves. Stems of pink starry flowers are produced in summer. The species with small rosettes which don't spread fast are particularly suitable for growing in containers, like *S. arachnoideum* with hairs like cobwebs.

Height × spread: 5 × 45cm/2in × 1 1/2ft

Soil: It needs sharply drained soil which is light and gritty.

Position: Plant in full sun amongst paving, in gravel, in containers or on walls.

Care: Deadhead. Divide in spring if needed.

○ ◊ E ❋❋❋

Sisyrinchium 'Quaint and Queer'

A curiosity amongst these dwarf rushy-leafed perennials, but worth growing for its small bronze flowers produced all summer on the end of wiry stems, among thin linear leaves. Some of these small species of sisyrinchium, though pretty, self-seed very freely and may invade the small garden. This includes the blue *S. graminoides* and the yellow *S. californicum*.

Height × spread: 30 × 30cm/1 × 1ft

Soil: Well-drained soil, even poor, which is neutral or with some lime.

Position: Plant in full sun in gravel or among paving.

Care: Watch that it does not suffer from too much rain in winter which could rot it.

| ◯ | ◊ | Semi-E | ❄❄❄ |

Stipa gigantea: Golden oats

A large grass can look dramatic on a patio as here. It forms evergreen clumps from which tall stems rise in early summer bearing lasting sprays of gold spikelets. Another species of ornamental grass that is attractive for a patio is *S. calamagrostis*, 1m/3ft tall, forming a thick tuft with stems carrying feathery purple spikelets.

Height × spread: 2 × 1m/6 × 3ft

Soil: For fairly fertile, light and well-drained soil.

Position: Plant in full sun, especially among paving as a specimen plant.

Care: Cut off the flowering stems at the end of the year. Divide if necessary in spring.

◯ ◊ ❘ E or Semi-E ❘ ❋❋❋

Tanacetum densum subsp. *amani*

One of the best silver-blue leafed, evergreen, woody perennials with yellow bobble daisies in summer which are sometimes cut off in favour of the foliage. It will form a small, low mound. It needs a sunny and warm position to thrive and dislikes excessive wet in winter. It can be increased by cuttings in spring. It tolerates poorish soil.

Height × spread: 25 × 20cm/10 × 8in

Soil: For well-drained light or sandy soil.

Position: Plant in a raised bed or rock garden or by paving, allowing for good drainage.

Care: Cut off the spent flower heads and tease out any old or rotted foliage in late winter.

◐ ◊ E ❋❋❋

Tulipa **'Blue Heron'**: Tulip

A tulip belonging to the fringed group with blue-mauve cup flowers with a marginal fringe to the petals. It blooms in spring. Other fringed tulips include the lemon 'Fringed Elegance' and the pink 'Bell Flower'. The bulbs may need lifting after dying down in the summer and re-planting in the autumn. In other gardens they persist to re-bloom well.

Height × spread: 45 × 7.5cm/1¹/₂ft × 3in

Soil: Plant in well-drained soil which is deep and fertile.

Position: Plant the bulbs in full sun in containers or in the border.

Care: Plant the bulbs deeply in autumn. Deadhead the spent flowers.

| ◯ | ◇ | ❋❋❋ |

Tulipa 'White Triumphator': Tulip

A beautiful pure white tulip belonging to the lily-flowered group, with an elegant and sometimes waisted shape to their blooms. These tulips flower in mid to late spring. Other good forms include the rose 'China Pink', yellow 'West Point' and the claret-coloured 'Burgundy'. In some gardens these bulbs may need lifting after dying down in summer, to be re-planted in autumn.

Height × spread: 60 × 7.5cm/2ft × 3in

Soil: They need well-drained soil which is deep and fertile.

Position: Plant in full sun in containers or in the border.

Care: Plant the bulbs deeply in autumn. Deadhead spent flowers.

| ○ | ◊ | ❄❄❄ |

Viola cornuta: Horned violet

An easy, spreading, low-growing viola with rich green leaves and spurred, white, violet or soft blue flowers from spring to summer covering this perennial plant. It will need pruning back after flowering to prevent straggliness. There are many viola hybrids which are excellent plants for the border front, like the blue and bronze-gold 'Ardross Gem'.

Height × spread: 15 × 30cm/6in × 1ft

Soil: Grow in fertile, moist but well-drained soil, rich in humus.

Position: Plant at the front of herbaceous beds or under roses in sun or dappled shade.

Care: Deadhead to extend flowering and prune back after flowering.

○ ◑ | ◊ | E | ❊❊❊

Viola labradorica: Labrador violet

A dwarf, self-sowing little perennial, never a nuisance even in small spaces. Soft purple flowers sprinkle the bronzed, dark green leaves in spring and more lightly in summer. *Viola* 'Bowles' Black' is another captivating self-sower though only an annual, with velvet flowers of the deepest purple-black with a golden eye. Both plants are fully hardy.

Height × spread: 7.5 × 15cm/3 × 6in

Soil: It tolerates most soils, but prefers humus-rich, moist but well-drained soil.

Position: Allow to self-sow in gravel, amongst paving gaps, or in small beds.

Care: None is required except for removing unwanted seedlings.

◯ ◑	◐	E	❋❋❋

Viola Sorbet Series

These biennials (or short-lived perennials) are wonderful in containers or when used for spring bedding. They have smaller flowers than the Universal Series of pansies which are often used for this purpose, but are prettier and also hardier. The flowers are bi-coloured in various shades of purple, lavender, gold, bronze and cream, with whiskered faces. The one in the photograph is 'Blackberry Cream'.

Height × spread: 10 × 20cm/4 × 8in

Soil: For fertile, moist but well-drained, humus-rich soil.

Position: For the front of beds or for containers of all kinds.

Care: Sow the seed in summer for winter to spring flowers. Deadhead to encourage continuity of bloom.

◖◗ ◊ ❋❋❋

Index of Common Names

E

F

G

H

I

J

K

L